THE BOOMERS' CAREER SURVIVAL GUIDE

THE BOOMERS' CAREER SURVIVAL GUIDE

Achieving Success and Contentment from Middle Age through Retirement

Ken Tanner

PRAEGER
An Imprint of ABC-CLIO, LLC

A B C CLIO

Santa Barbara, California • Denver, Colorado • Oxford, England

Library of Congress Cataloging-in-Publication Data

Tanner, Ken.
  The boomers' career survival guide : achieving success and contentment from middle age through retirement / Ken Tanner.
      p. cm.
  Includes index.
  ISBN 978-0-313-36521-8 (hard copy : alk. paper) — ISBN 978-0-313-36522-5 (ebook)
  1. Career changes. 2. Career development. 3. Baby boom generation—Employment. 4. Middle-aged persons—Employment. I. Title.
  HF5384.T36 2010
  650.1—dc22   2009034162

ISBN: 978-0-313-36521-8
EISBN: 978-0-313-36522-5

14 13 12 11 10   1 2 3 4 5

This book is also available on the World Wide Web as an eBook.
Visit www.abc-clio.com for details.

Praeger
An Imprint of ABC-CLIO, LLC

ABC-CLIO, LLC
130 Cremona Drive, P.O. Box 1911
Santa Barbara, California 93116-1911

This book is printed on acid-free paper (∞)

Manufactured in the United States of America

Note from the Author

I use a lot of stories in this book to illustrate the points I am making. Some of these stories are absolute fiction. These can be easily identified because they are about things like talking frogs or obviously made-up relatives. However, those stories in which I only use the character's first name are true, but either I was unable to contact the subject for permission or the person preferred not to be identified. In that case I not only changed the first name, but I also made changes to the location and some circumstances to protect their privacy. Other stories—those using a full name—are completely true in every respect; you can rely on them with the same credibility as you would the *New York Times*, MSNBC, or even Fox News.

Dedication

This effort is dedicated to:

Montine, my wife;

Almeda, Randy, Dan, and Jerry, my brothers- and sister-in-law;

Sunny, my sister;

Jeff, my editor, agent, publisher, and friend;

Mary, Jim, Ken, Kent, Brenda, Dave, Nick, Barbara, Big Al,
   and Zach, my good friends;

Jan, my lawyer;

Bryant, my pastor; and Inez, my recurring IRS agent;

Larry, Richard, Troy, "Mary Ann," Dale, Ralph, Gary,
   and Mary, my bosses and partners;

Peggy, my favorite writer;

Yo-Yo, my favorite musician;

Kelsey, my favorite actor;

Bill, George, and Barack, my presidents;

and to all the other 79,999,966 Boomers—thank you.

In the words of the great president during our generation,
   "Not bad. Not bad at all."

Contents

Acknowledgments

I have been blessed throughout this project by the skills of Michelle Moberg. When I first met Michelle, she was a 911 operator doing little except calming panicked people, guiding police chases, and occasionally saving lives. Despite the obvious importance of her job, Michelle still harbored an interest in developing her skills as a researcher, thus driving her participation in this book. She tracked down critical facts and opinions, conducted (excellent) interviews, and occasionally had to dig deep to uncover some obscure detail. That last duty sometimes led to some interesting dialog, such as the night I sent Michelle a text asking for her assistance.

> On the TV show GREEN ACRES what was Mr. Haney's first name?

> *That was 10 years before I was born. I'll have to pass on your trivia contest.*

> It's not trivia. It's for the book and you are the book's researcher. So research.

> *Oh. That's different. Can it wait a bit or do you want me to put this heart attack on hold?*

It's been fun watching Michelle grow. She has gone from a shy and private person to someone who eagerly seeks new ways to enrich herself and those around her. Besides all the work and encouragement (and nagging, BTW) she has given to me, Michelle has expanded her role dramatically with the public safety department of Eden Prairie, Minnesota. Most exciting, she is now enrolled to finish college, focusing on research and American history.

(You just watch, someday she'll write a bestseller on the lives of women during the Civil War.)

So thank you Michelle for your contributions. Your future is so very bright.

***

Also, very special thanks to: Lauren Azzalina, for assistance with the graphics; Panera Bread at The Avenue, East Cobb, for allowing me to camp out in their dining room while writing; Jeff Olson, for his wisdom, skill, and incredible patience; Katherine Tanner (my 12-year-old Millennial) for computer assistance; and Renae Tanner for her perspective on GenX career challenges as well as Montana whale laws.

Entr'acte

Technically, a Baby Boomer (hereafter referred to as a *Boomer*) is some-one born between 1946 and 1964. While these rather arbitrary dates actually do a fairly good job of grouping 80 million people who have a great deal in common, perhaps a better definition of Boomer can be found.

Try this one. A Boomer usually had parents that were raised during the Great Depression and experienced the Second World War as a young man or woman. How's that? No, that's more the definition of the Greatest Generation than Boomers. Let's try again.

Since we are all Boomers here, maybe we should have a more creative and fun definition. What about a Boomer checklist? Let's try this. Read through the following list. If most of the following phrases are vibrant in your memory then (with apologies to fellow Boomer Jeff Foxworthy) you may be a Boomer.

Girls named Betty, Jane, Pam, Sue, and Debbie
Boys named Robert, William, Richard, and Roger
Dippity Do, English Leather, and Green Goddess
A little dab will do ya, Jiffy Pop, penny candy
Hobos, beatniks, and hippies
Cool, groovy, far out, peace signs
Never trust anyone over 30. Flower Power
Burning draft cards; Burning bras; "Burn, baby, burn"
Avocado, coppertone, and burnt orange
Eight tracks, banana bikes, clothes lines

See the USA in your Chevrolet

Breaker, breaker, good buddy

Andy Griffith, Carol Burnett, Bob Newhart, and Mary Tyler Moore

Archie Bunker, Little Joe, Steve McGarrett, and Vinnie Barbarino

David Cassidy, Bobby Sherman, and Donny Osmond

Vinyl record albums, disco, and four channels on the TV

Up your nose with a rubber hose. Stifle it, Dingbat.

Shut up, Meathead. Eat my grits! Sock it to me!

Eastern, Pan-Am, TWA, and People Express

Stewardesses. Chicken, beef, or fish?

Polyester, bellbottoms, leisure suits, white belts and shoes

The slide rule, carbon paper, and the smell of a fresh mimeograph

Mini-skirts, hot pants, streaking, and ice trays

"By the year 2000 . . .", as well as "ice cream of the future."

I'd walk a mile for a Camel. Just a silly millimeter longer.

You're in Marlboro Country; Winston tastes good like a cigarette should;
    You've come a long way, baby; I'd rather fight than switch.

"Warning: Cigarette smoking may be hazardous to your health."

Ben Casey, Dr. Kildare, Trapper John, and Marcus Welby

Jethro, Mary Ann, Timmy, Beaver, and Opie

CONTROL, U.N.C.L.E, KAOS, the Mod Squad.

Rowan and Martin, Goober and Gomer, Chase and Sanborn, Bartles
    and James.

Mustang, Vega, Corvair, Pinto, along with my little GTO

Telling the gas station attendant, "Give me two dollars worth of
    regular"

Gas station attendants checking your oil and giving you a free bowl

Gas station attendants

Super Bowl halftime shows featuring *Up With People*

Houston Oilers, Baltimore Colts, New Orleans Jazz, and the Los
    Angeles Rams

The ABA, AFL, and WFL. Thanks Mean Joe

Great Taste! Less Filling! And Joe Namath in pantyhose.

Postage stamps for a nickel, Cokes for a dime, and gas 20 cents a
    gallon

Shag carpets, fallout shelters, pet rocks, and S&H Green Stamps.

Gay meant happy; Aids was a candy for dieters.

And rap meant you were taking the blame.

Red Skelton, Vida Blue, James Brown, Al Green, and the Man in Black

They call me Mellow Yellow. The Rainbow Coalition, Color My World

Goodnight Chet. Goodnight David. Goodnight, Johnboy.

"And that's the way it is . . ." *Heeeeere's Johnny!*

Bonus: Give the product specs for a McDonald's Big Mac sandwich. (Answer at the end of this section.)

In August of my 47th year, a tear stuck in my eye as I placed my six-year-old on the school bus for her first time. Feeling nostalgic, I then dropped into my neighborhood McDonald's and ordered my usual. When I looked at my receipt, the total was a bit less than I was normally charged. I was pleased with the gift until I discovered the reason. The Generation X cashier had given me the senior citizen's discount. In the space of 20 minutes I had gone directly from young adult to senior citizen, skipping right over middle age.

Life is like that for us Boomers in a lot of ways. Though our last three presidents are/have been Boomers, we still tend to think of leadership as being from the previous generation. We no sooner established our careers than we began to worry about GenXers (hereinafter often referred to as Jennifer and Christopher) pushing us "old geezers" aside. To paraphrase a character on the TV show *LA Law*, "I kept waiting for my life to start. Then on the morning of my fortieth birthday I realized that this was pretty much it."

While the fact is that we Boomers are in control of things, we really don't seem to realize it. In many ways we have been led to believe that our time quickly passed and it's time to step aside. Here's what I mean. We are often told that we are no longer within the advertisers' prime demographic group. It seems that ad agencies want their ads to appeal to the young folks, which they define as 18- to 39-year-olds. Have you ever wondered how that range came about, even though it makes little sense? (It makes little sense because most of the wealth, and therefore most of the disposable income, is held by adults age 45 through 70.)

It seems this advertising rule of thumb was created in the 1970s. At that time FOX didn't exist, and CBS dominated the news programming while NBC had the most viewers in prime time. ABC had no bragging rights whatsoever. So its creative gurus (Boomers no doubt) noticed that their lineup attracted a much younger audience than the other networks. ABC executives created this new demographic group and pounded away, convincing advertisers that this was the prime group to advertise to. The image stuck and soon began to be recognized as the prime ages for life in general, not just advertising. The myth began as a way to grab some extra ad dollars and eventually permeated how we think about just about everything. We have developed an inferiority complex of our own making.

In 2009 the youngest Boomers entered middle age and the oldest began to retire. Our generation—the largest, wealthiest, and most influential America has ever seen—is facing the most challenging time of our lives, the period from mid-career through retirement. Adding to your turmoil is a changed universe. Not only have your personal needs and desires changed since first entering the workforce, the work environment has become unrecognizable. We Boomers are confused, frightened, and looking for answers.

So here is the good news: Many of the fears are unfounded. Many perceived handicaps are actually assets. And there are wonderful opportunities hidden within this parade of Boomer crises. *The Boomers' Career Survival Guide* explains, addresses—and even celebrates—this period of our lives. It shows us how to understand the new paradigm, enjoy a satisfying career *now*, and prepare for the future *new* adventure of retirement. (To borrow from an Oldsmobile commercial—*This isn't your father's definition of retirement.*)

For the next couple of hundred pages, we're going to look at our generation's journey through the second half of our careers. We'll look at some real problems we have to face and creative ways to address them. We'll look at the new world we are in, how the rules have changed. And we'll realize that we can control far more of our destiny than we thought, as individuals as well as a group.

✳✳✳

Answer to Bonus Question: The product spec for a McDonald's Big Mac is:

Two all-beef patties, special sauce, lettuce, cheese, pickles, onions on a sesame seed bun. (Double the points if you can sing the tune.)

Part I

A Whirlwind of Change

After 20 years on Wall Street, Oliver left the pressures of Manhattan and bought a farm in Kansas. He arrived and, using the business skills he learned on Wall Street, immediately began analyzing the state of the business. There were several things needing upgrading but those could wait for a bit; however, there was one thing that had to be addressed immediately. Here, at a farm in Kansas in the heart of Tornado Alley, was a farm without a storm shelter. Oliver had recently seen the pseudo-documentary *Twister* and remembered the cows flying in front of the windshield (Or was it the same cow?). His experience told him this was a risk that must be addressed. Oliver installed a top-of-the-line storm shelter that was guaranteed to take a hit from a Korean-made nuke.

The day after it was installed, the clouds darkened, the temperature dropped, and the winds kicked up. Oliver grabbed his pet Arnold and ran into the shelter. After the noise died down he opened the door and took in the view. Everything was undisturbed. Birds were singing, the cows were grazing, and the flowers were brighter than ever.

A week later, the same conditions popped up. Oliver grabbed Arnold and headed to his shelter. An hour later he checked the landscape. Once again his farm looked like a postcard.

Five days later, the skies again darkened. Oliver and Arnold headed for shelter. An hour later he opened the door and surveyed the devastation. He viewed a yard full of assorted cow parts, his house a pile of toothpicks, and everything destroyed except cockroaches and a box of Twinkies. Oliver took a long breath and let it out slowly. "Well," he proclaimed. "Now that's more like it!"

It seems that we eventually get what we wish for, if we concentrate on it long enough. But, as we shall see, we must first learn to understand, react, and adapt to many things outside of our control. We've got to master our dealings with a whirlwind of changes.

Chapter 1

Changing

Let me offer a few more words and catchphrases Boomers might remember: *Sears Roebuck. What's good for General Motors is good for the nation. Middle management. Secretaries. Lifetime employment. Company loyalty. Employment security. Retirement.* Once omnipresent, these words and sayings are now either dead or so very close to the grave. We Boomers may have learned the hard way, but we have learned. Nothing stays the same. Even the continents drift.

When Boomers began our careers, the business place was a relatively stable place, at least in culture and the roles we all played. You applied for a job, answered some basic questions at the interview ("What are your strengths? Weaknesses? Tell me about yourself."), and then started on the bottom rung of the management structure. Eventually you grew into an office with a secretary. You did your job well and saw regular promotions and pay increases. You never worried about restructuring—layoffs were just for the blue-collar workers. You stayed on this track until age 65 at which point you retired with a good pension then laid down on the sofa until you had your heart attack.

Things have changed, considerably. Interviews are far more extensive, it's not unusual to change jobs every five years, and layoffs are now an equal-opportunity activity. You can no longer easily define the word "retirement," and a pension is an antique concept. And secretaries no longer exist.

The world we Boomers live in today looks little like the one we began our careers in. Not only does the world look different, the rules have changed. For instance, you are probably frustrated if you have been looking for a job using the same methods you used 20 years ago. Back then, your job search results were immediate and successful. Today you are getting nowhere and it has taken months just to get that far. You may have even tried to come into the 21st century and answered some ads from the Internet. All that has happened is that your mailbox fills up daily with advertisements for mortgages, diet pills, and various products guaranteeing greater sexual powers. These "overnight" changes have left the Boomer frustrated, perplexed, and just plain angry.

Industry is also having its own problems with change. It's no secret that foreign competition, technology, and rising costs are killing U.S. industries while others are trying to find ways to adapt. Here are 10 industries that are expected to see severe declines in revenue over the next several years. Some are rather obvious, but a few may surprise you.

bowling centers	textiles
music publishing	tobacco farming
laundry services	newspaper publishing
breweries	DVD Rental
wired telecoms	cemeteries

Yes, that's right. Cemeteries truly are a dying industry.

Actually the cemetery business is a good metaphor for all the other industries. It has been an accepted fact that there is nothing certain except death and taxes. (Now why couldn't *taxes* be the dying industry?) Based on this, you would think that there couldn't be a more stable industry than the business of burying people. Yet, even that has changed. Though life spans are lengthening and death is coming a lot later these days, death is still a certainty. But certain just isn't good enough. In a trend we didn't see coming even a decade ago, cremation is destroying the industry.

And that is the story of so many other industries in America. No, not that they're being affected by cremation, but that they are being attacked from directions they never anticipated. It's not unlike the French army, consistently ready to fight the last war. Just as corporations got really good at dealing with their problems, new ones attack. And industries are caught flat-footed.

The newspaper industry is another that may surprise you. I remember about a decade ago when newspaper Web sites began popping up on the Internet. This was followed by blogging. (Who could have predicted that blogs would make unknowns legitimate players in the news business?) There were predictions that these Internet sites would eventually replace the daily newspaper. I scoffed at the whole idea. A computer terminal could never replace a newspaper, I reasoned, because squinting at a terminal cannot replace the experience of sitting back in your favorite chair, sipping on a cup of coffee, and leisurely flipping through large pages. Also, what about the crossword puzzle? And, after all, you can't line a birdcage with a computer.

I guess you can figure out why my 401(k) is tanking. I'm pretty lousy with predictions. Newspapers are folding all over the country. Some, like the *Christian Science Monitor*, now only publish online. Our lifestyles have changed so that fewer and fewer people sip coffee in an easy chair, much less peruse a newspaper while they do it. We are surrounded by news sources, cable TV, satellite radio, Internet, even twittering (a medium I have thus far failed to embrace). And the news arrives immediately now, not the next day like with most newspapers. So many trends that we never saw coming have become integral to our lives.

And then some companies work hard and smart to identify The Next Great Trend. They make revisions to their business model, create a new product, sink millions into development, equipment, and marketing, and then still get bitten in the posterior. Let me tell you about one such company—a company that is normally used as an example of innovation and incredible management. At that time—1984 no less—it was known as Federal Express.

I had a good friend who was working for it at that time at its headquarters in Memphis. One day he pulled me aside and addressed me like he was a CIA operative. "Ken," he half whispered. "Go to the bank, pull out everything you've got, and buy Federal Express stock."

"Buy Federal Express stock?" I responded rather loudly. "What's up?"

"Shhhh! Keep your voice down." His eyes shifted back and forth, looking to see if anyone was eavesdropping. He continued. "We've discovered a miracle machine. You feed a document in one end. Then it makes a copy electronically, sends some beeps over a telephone line where it is then printed out on the other end. You will be able to send an exact copy of something from Memphis to San Francisco in about two minutes. That beats three-day mail by a long shot."

I was indeed impressed. "Wow. Business will eat this up. You guys will make a fortune selling these things."

"Sell them? No. Too expensive for anyone to buy, I'm sure. What we're going to do is put one in every Federal Express office in the country. People will flock in to their local office, send the document across the country, and the recipient can pick it up at the other end. Or we can deliver it by truck the next day."

"Seems like it would be faster to just send it as an overnight package," I observed.

"Yeah, that doesn't make sense. I guess they'll just go down to the office and pick up their ZapMail in person."

"ZapMail? Is that the name?"

"Yep. Cool name isn't it? Now get to your broker and stock up." My friend melted into the crowd. I told myself that this must have been how Deep Throat operated.

Federal Express did indeed launch ZapMail to great acclaim. It was a novel product that revolutionized the way business communicated. They had done a brilliant job of anticipating future needs and capitalizing on that future trend. Unfortunately, the company invested $300,000,000 in this great business before calling it quits.

What happened? True, Federal Express had done an amazing job of analyzing the market and understanding trends. There was most certainly a demand for this product, but the demand was far greater than Federal Express anticipated. People loved the service so much that businesses rushed to buy their own fax machines. At first each business owned one, then a fax was purchased for each floor. Eventually you could find a fax machine in individual offices as well as many homes. There was no longer a need for ZapMail. Federal Express had been too darn successful.

(Fortunately, I had no money in the bank so I didn't load up on Federal Express stock. Today I wonder what had happened if the company had followed my initial reaction and just gotten into the business of selling the machines.)

AND YOU HAVE CHANGED

Your career path today is much different than it was at the beginning of your career. Consider:

- You are no longer considered a (*shudder!*) job hopper if you change jobs every three or four years.
- Lifetime employment only exists for people with very short lives.
- We are now totally responsible for our own careers.

Let's address the chicken or egg question. Who was the first to abandon loyalty, the corporation or labor? My theory is that it was the corporation that first rejected loyalty, soon followed by the employee as a defensive measure. Some management guru was able to inject his disruptive theory into traditional corporate culture in the late 1980s. Rather than working towards a stable labor force, companies discovered the short-term benefits of layoffs and company reorganizations. Since the notion of "loyalty in exchange for lifetime employment" no longer made bottom-line sense to many organizations, hundreds of thousands of workers lost their jobs. For the first time, white-collar employees were as vulnerable as their blue-collar counterparts. And stock prices could be temporarily and artificially boosted by announcement of the plans to downsize.

So, like the falling of dominos, management's abandonment of loyalty begot labor's knowledge that it had to take care of itself. In other words, it was at this point that employees recognized that the only one who would look after their career was the employee himself. Note—and this is important—this change occurred in the middle of most Boomer careers. We grew up under one set of rules and now we experience an alternate paradigm. Because of this, we often try to face today's problems with yesterday's solutions. It just doesn't work. And this is why so many of us are confused and frustrated. *It worked before, why not now?* we ask.

How do we bridge this gap between the past and today's reality? We can only do this by realizing that in today's world, your career will be dead in the water unless you become self-reliant and take charge of your own career destiny.

COPING WITH CHANGE

Our personal lives change as we grow older, why should our careers be any different? Denial will only make your life and career more difficult. Understanding that change will happen makes you better prepared for that inevitable change. Here are some points to help you deal with the constant changes we experience as Boomers.

Give Change a Chance. It's inevitable anyway so you might as well embrace it. Do your part to make things happen and observe how things affect you. Note that most change will enhance the value of your job and increase your job security.

Embrace Change. It's coming, it's here, and it's coming again. We need to understand that change is not only inevitable, but it will actually make our careers more fulfilling in the long run.

Be Flexible. Demonstrate a willingness to take on new responsibilities. Failure to do this might give you the reputation of being the old dog who refuses to learn new tricks. Asking for additional responsibilities show that you are on the team. Management is watching closely during times of change and you don't want to get labeled as an attitude problem.

Take Responsibility for Your Career. The reality of the workplace today is that jobs are not guaranteed and neither is stability. Identify what's important to your career and then take action. Track down this new training you may need and then grab it. This does not mean you need to go back to college for another degree. Most colleges, especially local community colleges, offer continuing education courses targeted at adults who need to brush up on old skills or learn new ones. Most also offer Internet courses that allow you to complete course work at home and on your own schedule.

Such classes typically require only a few hours per week and cost as little as $150. Call up your local college and ask for a catalog of course options.

Communication is what makes the process of change work—for the company as well as for you. Use your job skills to understand what is happening and to have an impact on making it work the best it can.

View Change as an Opportunity, Not a Threat. Use change to your advantage, and look for ways it can be used to improve the product, streamline how the product is produced, or better serve your clients. An environment that is comfortable with change is a culture where problems can be addressed.

Change Breeds Change. Changes tend to beget more changes. Like a branching tree, one change will multiply exponentially. A single change requires adjustments in many other areas. There will be many opportunities for you to monitor and build on the ancillary issues. Approach these offshoots in a positive manner, but do use your expertise to help deal with any unintended consequences. It's your opportunity to be a hero in the eyes of management. (Or, if handled poorly, a chance to be seen as a stubborn grandparent.)

See the Big Picture. Focusing only on the one change that will be made causes you to not see the reasons it was made. Develop a management perspective, look at the horizon, and understand why the change was made. Often we find that the important goals have not really changed, only the tactics used to get there have.

CONQUERING CHANGE BY ANTICIPATING THE FUTURE

I've spent some time now talking about how to catch up with change. But many of you want to do better than that—rather than reacting to change, how about anticipating change? If we can do that, we can get ahead of the curve. We can be in control! The wild card in this plan is being able to predict what those trends toward change will be. As anyone who has been humbled by trying to predict the market can tell you, it is very difficult to make accurate predictions.

Here is an excerpt from the *Ladies Home Journal* from December 1900. This article attempted to predict the world of 2000. Consulting leading scientists and businessmen of the day, the *Ladies Home Journal* gathered 100 special forecasts of the world 100 years hence. Here are some examples:

> *Prediction #2:* The American will be taller by from one to two inches. He will live fifty years instead of thirty-five as at present—for he will reside in the suburbs.
>
> *Prediction #4:* There Will Be No Street Cars in Our Large Cities. All hurry traffic will be below or high above ground when brought within city limits. Cities, therefore, will be free from all noises.

Prediction #7: There will be air-ships, but they will not successfully compete with surface cars and water vessels for passenger or freight traffic.

Prediction #9: Photographs will be telegraphed from any distance. If there be a battle in China a hundred years hence snapshots of its most striking events will be published in the newspapers an hour later. Even to-day photographs are being telegraphed over short distances. Photographs will reproduce all of Nature's colors.

Prediction #11: Mosquitoes, houseflies and roaches will have been exterminated.

Prediction #12: Peas as Large as Beets.

Prediction #16: There will be No C, X or Q in our every-day alphabet. They will be abandoned because unnecessary.

Prediction #17: A university education will be free to every man and woman. Several great national universities will have been established.

Prediction #18: Telephones Around the World. Wireless telephone and telegraph circuits will span the world. A husband in the middle of the Atlantic will be able to converse with his wife sitting in her boudoir in Chicago. We will be able to telephone to China quite as readily as we now talk from New York to Brooklyn.

Prediction #19: Grand Opera will be telephoned to private homes, and will sound as harmonious as though enjoyed from a theatre box.

Prediction #21: Hot and Cold Air from Spigots. Hot or cold air will be turned on from spigots to regulate the temperature of a house as we now turn on hot or cold water from spigots to regulate the temperature of the bath.

Prediction #23: Ready-cooked meals will be bought from establishments similar to our bakeries of today. They will purchase materials in tremendous wholesale quantities and sell the cooked foods at a price much lower than the cost of individual cooking. Food will be served hot or cold to private houses in pneumatic tubes or automobile wagons.

Prediction #28: There will be no wild animals except in menageries. Rats and mice will have been exterminated. The horse will have become practically extinct.

While there were some pretty good guesses, a huge majority of these experts predictions were quite off-course. And more than a half-century later, the batting average got even worse. The 1964 New York World's Fair dazzled visitors with visions of a bright future aided by technology. General Motors (GM) *Futurama* exhibit showed a city 10,000 feet under the ocean reached by atomic submarines. There was also a lunar colony and pumps sending ocean water to deserts. Cars drove themselves along automated highways. (Oddly, the GM exhibit failed to predict its own demise.)

BAD PREDICTIONS

Here are some predictions that were a bit off:

- "Inventions have long since reached their limit, and I see no hope for further developments," Roman engineer Julius Sextus Frontinus, A.D. 10.
- "Despite the trend to compactness and lower costs, it is unlikely everyone will have his own computer any time soon," Reporter Stanley Penn, *The Wall Street Journal*, 1966
- "By the turn of this century, we will live in a paperless society," Roger Smith, chairman of General Motors, 1986.

Careers of the Future?

So, there you have some of the predictions made in 1900 for what the world would be like in the year 2000. Some of these predictions were amazingly spot on, other were terribly off base. (What happened to all the flying cars?)

There are many gurus predicting the hot careers of the future. Here are the cream of those predictions and a summary of the logic for their urging you to prepare for these "wonderful" opportunities.

computational biology	brain analysts
parallel programming	space tourism
simulation engineering	roboticists

Just like the *Ladies Home Journal*, some of these predictions will definitely be correct. Others will be laughed at 20 years from today. But here's the problem: how can you know which is which? If you are just playing a mental game and just seeing how good of a prognosticator you are, then no harm is done. But if you are thinking about using a list such as this to shape the rest of your career, well then we have serious risk.

Let me make my own set of predictions of some of the hot careers for the next 20 years.

law enforcement officers	consultants
attorneys	sales
physicians	teachers
contractors	nurses
managers	electricians

And of course we'll need mechanics—to work on all those flying cars. Here is my point: true, the world is changing and careers are changing but, despite the whirlwinds, many basics remain. As you analyze what to do with the second half of your career, realize that while you do have to adapt, you do not need to put your life at risk. Switching careers? It makes much more sense to become a high school math teacher than to roll the dice in the "emerging" space travel industry.

New jobs have been created that didn't exist when you were 25. Among the hottest fields is computer programming. No, wait a second. Since I wrote that sentence computer programming has gone from being the hottest new profession to one that is overpopulated. But here is my prediction. Like engineers and teachers, the availability of programming jobs will be cyclical. If it is your field of choice, stay with it.

Chapter 2

Coping

There is a unique pottery shop located in a small historical town in eastern Tennessee. Inside you will find the usual pottery items—bowls, plates, cups, and other usable décor, all of extremely high quality. What makes the shop unique is the owner and artist who mines and mixes his own mud and creates his art on the premises. For several hours a day, Brother John sits in a dirty little corner, spinning the mud into quite beautiful accessories for the home and office.

I had the good fortune to drop in to the shop at a time when Brother John was at work. We struck up a conversation, and he soon revealed himself to be one of the most interesting fellows I've met. It seems John had been operating his shop in the same location since 1973, right after he had returned from Vietnam and spent the obligatory two years as a hippie in San Francisco. The hippie years left a strong impression on him as he still dresses like the 1960s Haight-Ashbury crowd, has a long flowing beard, and remains a vegetarian. ("Except when I cheat and have a barbecue sandwich, about once a day," he added with a wink.)

Brother John spoke lovingly about his wife, whom I think he met at some tree-huggers' rally, and his GenX son, John Junior. (I didn't ask the most obvious question, since he was a "junior" was his birth name also "Brother" John? Or would it be "Son" John. Perhaps I digress.)

He learned that I was in the "career business" and shared an aggravation with me. Brother John had spent over 30 years building his shop and a great reputation. "It's known all over the South," he added with justifiable pride, "and generates some impressive income." It seems that Brother John had spent many years training and prepping Junior in the craft and learning the business, in the certainty that he would eventually take over

---

HOW MANY BOOMERS ARE THERE?

Depending on how it is calculated, there are 76, 72, or 80 million of us. Why the complication? There were actually 76 million births in the United States between 1946 and 1964. Of the 76 million born, about 4 million had died by the time Census 2000 was taken, leaving some 72 million survivors.

But as they say in the infomercials, "Wait, there's more!" Census 2000 counted 80 million U.S. residents born in the years 1946 to 1964, inclusive. That number is higher than the 76 million births because net immigration outweighed deaths.

Here is the reason for the flood of statistics. Throughout this book you will see various numbers mentioned for the populations of different generations and they may not be consistent. That is because I used varying sources for the different sections and they got their numbers from even more varying sources. While I could go back and make all the numbers consistent, I simply chose to leave the them in their original form. In no case did the differing numbers change the meaning of the point being made.

---

the family business. But Junior had a bit of Alex P. Keaton in him. "My boy went off to college and planned on majoring in fine arts. But then those neo-con professors got ahold of him and convinced him to go another direction. Before you know it, John's got his accounting degree and now he's a financial advisor in Charlotte. Damn-it-all!"

I was a bit taken aback, this being my first time to be captured in a parallel universe. Shaking my head, I managed to utter some brilliant philosophy, "Kids. What can you do?"

"Yep. What can you do?" he quietly replied.

COPING WITH THE OTHER GENERATIONS

Let's explore the *generation gap,* a term that we Boomers coined in the late 1960s. When we invented this term we were only referring to our parents' inability to understand us. But today a different spin can be taken. Now it really refers to the difficulty relating, communicating, and understanding the two generations who follow us in the workplace. We Boomers have spent our lives exploring our inner id; perhaps we could improve our environment by gaining insight into GenX as well as the Millennials. At the time, we thought the gap between our parents and us was huge, but the one between the younger two generations and us is even wider. This is because our world has changed so much in the last 50 years, and it does seem every generation forever views the world through 30-year-old eyes. A good example—when referring to communication skills, we Boomers might think of formal writing and speaking abilities; a Millennial would probably think of e-mailing and text messaging.

A Quick Glance at Ourselves, the Boomers Born between 1946 and 1964, 80 Million in Population

We've already discussed many of the traits we have in common, but let's do a quick review of those traits we see in the workplace. We'll use these traits to contrast us with the other two generations, which we'll look at in some detail.

Since we grew up with approximately 80 million peers, we have developed into a highly competitive generation. We have the reputation that we live to work and that we are willing to sacrifice almost anything to achieve success. This is reflected in the skyrocketing divorce rates as well as a coolness in some family relationships. (Again, this is compared to the generation that came before us and the two that have followed.)

Recognition, respect, and reputations are important to Boomers. While rebellion and challenging authority are two of the hallmarks of our generation, Boomer bosses just won't tolerate the same from the younger groups. Like the predecessor generation, Boomers favor a top-down approach and are sensitive about being shown respect. On the other hand we like to communicate in a personable manner, like to build rapport, and will attempt to solve a lot of problems by calling meetings. We can also take credit for knocking down walls of formality in the workplace, reshaping corporate culture with casual dress codes, calling people by their first names, integrating women into positions of leadership, and establishing flexible schedules.

A Peek at the GenXers Born between 1965 and 1979, Approximately 60 Million in Population

For the most part, GenXers are the children of Boomers. So much of their career profile is either because of or in rebellion to that parentage. The Boomer's high divorce rate combined with the explosion in the number of moms who worked meant many GenXers grew up as latchkey kids. Left on their own, GenXers learned how to take care of themselves. This led to traits of independence, resilience, and adaptability. They will tell you quite bluntly, "I don't need anyone looking over my shoulder."

They also saw how much their Boomer parents sacrificed their lives for their careers. In addition they witnessed their parents agonize over their job security in the 1980s recession. Many of them also entered the workplace at that time and had an early experience with that very same agony. Because of these factors, GenXers are often skeptical and individual workers who put a premium on a work/life balance.

Generation X grew up in a culture of instant results—from remote controls to the birth of the Internet. They value efficiency and directness. Expectations are for immediate and instantaneous communication.

We Boomers can best relate and communicate with them by being direct, cutting to the chase, and not calling a lot of meetings. They expect immediate and regular feedback, and are equally comfortable giving feedback to others.

GenXers define loyalty differently than we do. Boomers consider loyalty as something directed at the company while a GenXer is committed to their co-workers and their career. While Boomers consider ourselves Cubs, Lakers, or Falcons, GenXers are third basemen, point guards, and linebackers.

GenX dislikes authority and arbitrary work requirements even more than we do. (They got that rebellious streak from us.) So how should we go about developing a mentoring relationship with them? First of all, the relationship must be as hands-off as possible. Provide immediate and direct feedback. Encourage their creativity and use of their creative problem solving skills. Have the GenX protégé work with you, not for you. Remember they work best when they're given the desired goal and then turned loose to figure out how to achieve it on their own.

A Peek at the Millennials Born between 1980 and 2000, Approximately 75 Million in Population

The 75 million members of this generation are being raised at the most child-centric time in our history. Millennials were raised by younger Boomers and a few older GenXers. This mixed lineage has given this generation a unique perspective on life and career. Most people think the Millennials are nothing more than younger versions of GenXers, but that is not turning out to be the case at all. Actually, in many ways, Millennials are closer to Boomers than Xers. (And as a father of two GenXers and one Millennial, I can verify the truth to that!)

Millennials do share the GenXers feelings about a work/life balance; however, they differ in that Millennials are generally optimistic and highly collaborative. They've been taught to put feelings on the table. It would be smart to present them with news and other messages in a positive light.

Unlike the Boomers and the GenXers, this generation grew up routinely using technology. Because of this, technology comes natural to them (unlike Boomers and the GenXers, who may become proficient in the newest technology but will always consider it a second language).

While Millennials are typically self-confident (almost cocky), they are also team-oriented. They work well in groups, preferring collaborative efforts to individual endeavors. They're good multitaskers, having juggled sports, school, and social interests as children, so expect them to work hard. Millennials respect positions and titles and expect structure in the workplace. While this works well in dealing with Boomers, it doesn't always mesh with GenX's independence and hands-off style.

Of course all we know or theorize about Millennials is based, as they say on election night, on the "early returns." The older Millennials are just dipping their toes in the workforce while the youngest are in elementary school. Many things could yet occur to our nation, the economy, technology, or even their parents that could have a major impact on the Millennial perspective.

Understanding these two generations gives us Boomers a head start in being able to relate to them and communicate our mutual thoughts. Just like Boomers, individual members of these generations are not copies of one another. Each member has her own personality or approach and that should certainly be the main factor in you relationship. Still it is interesting how, as a group, the GenXers, Millennials, and of course us Boomers, have rather distinct personalities, priorities, and perspectives. Use these abstracts as a starting point to understand the individuals.

COPING WITH AGE DISCRIMINATION

Many experts say that age discrimination is the new civil rights movement for us Boomers. Other experts state uncategorically that age discrimination is a myth, nothing more than an excuse unsuccessful people use as a crutch to explain why they didn't get a job or a promotion. Me? I stand firmly with the experts.

It is ironic that we Boomers are complaining about discrimination against older workers, since we spent our early career years doing just that as hiring managers, as well as being the beneficiary of just such discrimination as employees. And now that we are the older workers, we're still doing it. "The worst age discrimination I've seen is done by older managers," says the principal in one of the nation's top recruiting firms (who needs to stay anonymous for obvious reasons). Perhaps this is because they have spent their whole careers avoiding the hiring of older workers. We Boomers created the very culture that is now biting our own rear ends. As we say in Georgia, *Payback's hell, ain't it?*

So what does the law say? Under the federal Age Discrimination in Employment Act, workers 40 and over cannot be arbitrarily discriminated against because of age in employment decisions, including hiring. Yep, that's what it says. But the law also says women are to get equal pay, you can't cross the U.S. border without the proper documents, and you are not allowed to bring a whale into the state of Montana. With the possible exception of the whale-thingie, some laws just aren't enforced. In fact, it's rather hard to enforce many of them. How do you prove intent? How do you even know for sure that it was age that knocked out the applicant?

While it is tough to prove discrimination when you find patterns, it is nearly impossible to do so for individual isolated cases. Unless the employer actually confesses or makes an incriminating statement like the recruiter mentioned earlier, you really can't determine which factor was the one that caused a candidate to be passed over.

COME ON, IS IT REALLY DISCRIMINATION?

We Boomers need to be careful throwing out charges of discrimination. Loosely using a word makes it lose its meaning. (Like "superstar" or "wrinkle-free.")

I once had the good fortune to do some recruiting for the Hooter's restaurant chain. Unfortunately, my assignment was for management, not waitresses. I followed with great interest a claim that Hooter's was discriminating against men because the company only hired women as waitresses. The U.S. Equal Employment Opportunity Commission (EEOC) decided to play hard ball and force the company to hire men as servers. Hooter's beat the federal government through public pressure after running ads showing a hairy Hooter's man in one of the company's trademark skimpy outfits. The feds, finally realizing the silliness of their venture, eventually dropped the claim.

There's a perception that people over 50 will be just passing through as they transition into retirement. Employers are loathe to hire someone who they think will be out the door in a year or two. Now this logic may violate the *letter* of the law, but in my book it does not violate the spirit of the law. It's a projected tenure question, not age. As we discuss in chapter 10, even a 60-year-old Boomer can plan on staying on the job for another 10 or 15 years. Solution? Applicants should be asked about those plans rather than assuming their future tenure.

I had an uncomfortable situation once. I was doing a phone interview with a man who had some very impressive credentials if he were early in his career. However if he were further along in his career the experience would have been a bit shallow for the high position I was hiring for. I decided to cut to the chase. "How old are you?" I asked impetuously. There was a long silence on the other end of the phone, then he firmly replied, "It's illegal for you to ask me that question." I answered him in my best Lou Grant voice, "Wanna call a cop?" The funny thing is that this man was 34 years old and—for that age—had extraordinary experience. And that fact would have worked firmly in his favor. But he blew the interview because he chose to make a big deal over something that wasn't even a problem. (The law doesn't cover workers under 40.) But even if it had been a problem, don't openly fight such questions. You will never win that argument.

Fighting Discrimination

A computer programmer with excellent credentials spoke with a headhunter about a position that he seemed a perfect fit for. The recruiter told him he was too old to change jobs. His age? Fifty-one. This story is repeated many times a day as Boomers are faced with a culture that seems to declare them over-the-hill at midlife.

What about a lawsuit? Usually not a successful venture. If an employee already works at a company, he or she may have a chance to gather evidence of discrimination but that's generally not possible for workers applying for jobs. You will simply not be able to isolate the discrimination. How can you prove what is going through the interviewers head? Even if he does have a slip of the tongue, he will of course deny it. Even then, how do you know that your failure to get a job was because of your age or because of some other criterion? No matter how tempting, it is just not in your interest to haul the employer before EEOC or a court of law. EEOC prefers to gather groups for large cases and the process in a court would take a case like this a dozen years. It's almost like having another career, except you don't get paid and it doesn't look good on your resume.

However, the Supreme Court opened up an intriguing possibility in 2005 by declaring that age discrimination did not have to be intentional for it to be real. For instance I know of an organization that could be in hot water even though it most certainly did not intentionally discriminate by age. How can I be so sure? Over half of their staff was over 40 and over half of the people they hired were over 40. So what's the problem? The problem was that a new training program had resulted in a large number of terminations in the first year. And *all* of those terminations were for people over 40 years old. Clearly, unintentional discrimination occurred.

So what should these employees have done, file suit? Again, that is not my recommendation for the reasons mentioned previously. However I would call a meeting with management and HR. I'd lay out the pattern, explain the law, and urge a new look at the training program along with the rehiring of those affected. If the organization is truly concerned about discrimination, they'll be eager to work out a fair solution. Really.

Overqualified?

Boomers have told me that they are often told that they are overqualified while interviewing for a job. I have one question for the person who uses that term: *What in the living hell does overqualified mean?* It simply makes no sense! Would you reject a brain surgeon who seemed to know too much? How about an overqualified firefighter who's about to run in to your burning house and save your child? Better yet do you tremble in your seat agonizing over the possibility that the pilot of your airplane has too much experience? Of course not. So why would anyone refuse the services of anyone for the reason that she has too much experience? Ignorance, pure friggin' ignorance.

Let me tell you what someone means when they say you are overqualified. They are saying you are too old and the job is at a level you passed by a long time ago. So why are they concerned about your age? Here is what is really on their minds:

You Have a Lack of Energy. Employers worry about the stereotypes associated with age. They sometimes assume that if you are "over the hill" (by their definition) that you are beset by arthritis, suffering from Alzheimer's, and probably gargle Geritol at lunch. Make it clear by your actions that you do not have an energy shortage. Now by that I don't mean that you should behave as a frenzied otter, but I do mean that you should be alert, maintain good eye contact, and never, ever yawn. (Actually yawning can be prevented. Since it is a product of low oxygen levels, simply take regular full breaths. Or one really deep one.) Take this issue off the table by your actions.

You Want to Get Your Foot in the Door and Take Away Their Job. This is always a worry of an insecure younger manager who is interviewing you for a job below your previous level. So level with him. Explain that you have no desire to return to the previous level. You see in this job everything you really want in your career and would be quite happy doing it. Shape the conversation so he doesn't worry that your real intention is to squish him and take his office.

You Are Just Going to Stick Around Until You Find Something Else. Again, if this job is below your normal level, the interviewer is going to be suspicious. And she'll have every right to be. Many people who are having trouble finding that "right" job go out and grab any job just so they'll have some income while looking for something better. What do you do? Just as with the previous situation, be prepared to explain the reasons you want this specific position.

You Won't Respect Your Younger Boss. We spend a lot of time discussing younger bosses in chapter 6, but for now let me suggest this. Prove to her that you will indeed treat her with respect by doing so during the interview. Ask her opinions and ask for information. Be careful to avoid patronizing the hiring manager. If you are condescending, you'll have the opposite effect and only confirm her fears.

There is one area in which the applicant hears the "O" word a lot. When you are looking to change careers it is typical that you may begin several levels below your normal career station. It's important that you explain this to the interviewer so that she doesn't just assume you are trying to find a temporary job.

Another assumption she may have is that you simply made a mistake and thought there was more to the job. Quite frankly, this may be the truth, we often see job titles that are inflated and that can certainly mislead applicants. To prevent that embarrassment, thoroughly investigate a job before applying. Make sure you understand what the job entails. But if you have done that and are genuinely interested in the job, sell the interviewer on the fact. Welcome the "overqualified" statement as your opportunity to explain exactly why you want that job and how it fits into your career. Emphasize your skills, not titles. Explain how you will get along with the coworkers, explain how the salary will meet your needs, and enthusiastically tell her how the job will indeed keep you challenged.

And if all else fails, be direct. Ask her, "What can I say to convince you I am the best person for this job?" Have her describe the ideal candidate, and then, point by point, explain how you fit that profile.

❊❊❊

Is age discrimination fair? Of course not. But who promised life would be fair? If life were fair, Elvis would be alive and all the impersonators would be dead. The fact is there are some companies out there that do blatantly discriminate against Boomers. Despite the unfairness of it all, you are much better off not fighting them. Instead, seek out the many companies that welcome your experience, work ethic, and maturity.

Interviewing for Boomers

Since we opened the door with the discussion of handling the "overqualified" remark, we're going to go ahead and jump ahead of ourselves a bit. While it would seem that the subject of handling interviews might fit better in chapters 7 or 8, it will flow nicely right here. (And we will get back to the subject in detail in chapter 7; rest assured.) That's because the big worry for Boomers during job interviews is that they are labeled "old." So we'll focus on age as we prepare ourselves to talk with potential employers.

We Boomers have one thing working against us at interviews—our age. But more importantly we have one thing working for us—our experience. Your objective at a job interview is to convert age questions into experience answers.

The age prejudices that some employers have are really not about gray hair, it's more subtly hidden. Employers worry about energy level, ambition, and flexibility. So, while you will only rarely get a question that is directly about your age, you are apt to get bombarded with questions probing age-related traits. Let's study some of the more common ways the issue may be addressed.

Don't Look Old. You only get one chance to make a first impression. (No, I didn't make that up.) Look professional and up-to-date, but don't go to the extreme and dress like a 25-year-old. Men, beards make you look older, even if isn't full of gray hair. Shave it off. And never even consider dying your hair. (A 60-year-old with jet-black hair looks like an 80-year-old with jet-black hair.) Women, no clunky jewelry, strong perfumes, or frumpy clothing. And no short skirts or low-cut dresses either.

Be Up-to-Date with Pop Culture. Although I admit my favorite television program is *The Andy Griffith Show*, my favorite president was Gerald Ford, and I remember my Pinto with great fondness (until it blew up), I would never bring any of that up at an interview. Just speak in the language of the day. It's a good idea to read *USA Today* to stay aware of the most current social happenings.

Avoid Old-Fogeyisms. Don't ever talk about "how we used to do it," or use the phrase, "in the good old days." Don't mention that as time goes by you "seem to be attending more and more funerals." Don't discuss your health and especially don't mention that you are worried about your prostate or hot flashes. Good rule of thumb: *Don't be your parents.*

Dress Well. Just because you are older doesn't mean that you should present a frumpy, older image to the world. Instead, continue to update your style and fashion sense so that it continues to reflect a professional, up-to-date image. Don't try to copy the styles that are possibly unsuited to your age but do keep your existing wardrobe abreast of current trends and styles.

Show You Are Eager to Learn. Give recent examples of your willingness—no, make that *eagerness*—to learn new skills. Explain that you consider yourself a lifetime learner and give examples of your attending classes at a community college or participating in learning events.

Emphasize That You Understand Technology. The interviewer will assume that as a Boomer the only thing you can do on a computer is play solitaire and all you know about modern technology is that a microwave is lousy for toasting bread. Sorry, but people do tend to exaggerate stereotypes. The best way to show that your skills are current is to reflect it on the resume and in the answers to her questions. Make it obvious that you are as current in technology as any whippersnapper.

Don't Put a Spotlight on Your Age. Don't show off pictures of your grandkids, brag about the discounts you get using your AARP card, or mention that you worked in the Nixon campaign. And never use the word "whippersnapper."

Use Examples. The best way to show your deep experience is with colorful stories. Stories convey your message much more memorably than a recitation of cold facts or statistics. Remember employers look at your past performance to predict your future performance. Pepper the conversation with stories about how you found a way to improve customer service, cut expenses, or dealt with a particularly nasty employee situation.

Emphasize Adaptability. Many people have the perception that Boomers are set in their ways and resistant to new things. Demonstrate—again through stories—that you are open to new ideas and eager to try new things.

Explain That You Intend to Mentor. Turn age into and asset by emphasizing your intention to mentor younger workers. Let them know hiring you means far more than just seeing you do a good job, you'll also enhance the productivity and culture of the workplace.

Answer the Question, "What Are Your Career Goals?" What they really want to know is, "How many years before you retire?" Make it clear that you plan on working indefinitely because you love what you do. If they actually bring up retirement, respond incredulously, *"Retirement*? It's a long time before I'll even be thinking about that." Or if the situation allows it, use a little humor, "I'll make you this guarantee. Give me this job and I'll serve a minimum of ten years. You can't get that kind of commitment even out of a presidential candidate."

The Future Definition of Age Discrimination

Now here is something that will make you chuckle. I'm sure you noticed the tremendous drop off in the number of GenXers compared from the number of Boomers. From about 80 million to about 60 million—a full 25 percent! There are many ramifications to this population implosion. One positive effect, at least for the Boomers, is the employment opportunities created as Boomers begin to retire.

Even though Boomers leave the workforce, the jobs remain. Someone has to step into those jobs Boomers leave and there are just not enough GenXers to do so. And though it might appear that the Millennials can close the gap, remember that they are too young in their careers to make up for the experience we Boomers leave on the table.

So what are the ramifications of this? Some jobs will simply be left empty. If this problem cannot be addressed with other workers, then the United States must fill the gap with technology, immigration, or a significant drop in productivity. Then again, many of these jobs will be filled by GenXers or even a few Millennials. While the headcount may break even, the experience has been lost. This loss in intellectual capital would have a severe economic and social impact.

But we'll actually solve this problem thanks to the same group that caused it—us. As the older Boomers leave the workforce, the younger Boomers will move into those senior positions. Further, a worker shortage means opportunity for those wanting to work part-time or start their own business. Unintentionally, we Boomers have acted as an 80 million member team to help ourselves while solving this great economic issue for the country.

Age discrimination is about to take on a whole new meaning. As experienced workers suddenly become scarce, their value skyrockets. Instead of rejecting them, employers will be seeking more Boomers. The more experienced the better. Age discrimination will no longer refer to older workers, it will soon have the younger inexperienced worker as its target. Strange how these things happen.

We need to recognize this important fact: age has its job-related advantages. What the older workers lack in raw physical ability, they make up in their ability to avoid the kind of problems that require reflexes and strength to solve. We are more reliable, less volatile, and generally more productive than our younger colleagues.

With all the changes in technology and work culture, physical performance is seldom a serious issue in the modern workplace. Most jobs are desk jobs. The single biggest advantage of youth—strength—is no longer a big factor on the job. Jobs that require real-life intellectual performance demand the kind of intellectual/experiential/analytical mix that peaks in a person's fifties.

It's often said that we don't really appreciate something until we are about to lose it. Maybe that philosophy now applies to Boomers. So many factors combine to prove the worth of Boomers. And now, with the impending labor shortage, employers are about to appreciate us a lot.

COPING WITH BOOMER DEMONS

There is a day that eventually comes to many of us. It is the day where you suddenly realize that you will never be the second baseman for the Boston Red Sox. Or it dawns on you that it's too late to join the Air Force or train for the Olympics or win a Nobel Prize. You'll never be in a rock band, star in a movie, or—and this one really eats at you—be president of the United States. All those dreams and fantasies you had as a child and as a young adult have passed you by. You are not going to be the superstar you just knew you would be. You are going to have to settle for being the best pork salesman in northeast South Dakota, the smartest professor at Siler City Community College, or a vice chair of the liquor control board for the state of Utah. And for that moment, it's just not good enough.

Lots of movies have used this as a great plot, such as the classic It's a Wonderful Life. Funny, when you see it on the screen it is so obvious that Jimmy Stewart was having an incredible life, but when you are in his shoes, things just plain suck.

AN IMPORTANT CONSIDERATION

Many of the symptoms of a mid-career crisis or job burnout are also indicators for clinical depression. Depression is an illness and is totally out of my competency to diagnose or offer help. Depression is a common condition and is treatable. If you think you are possibly dealing with depression, please visit your physician.

That, my friends, is a mid-life crisis. And the equivalent emotions are felt in the mid-*career* blues (often occurring at the same time). How does this condition erupt? Two words—boredom and emptiness.

Boredom

It is the same routine, day after day. Maybe you are not screwing the same bolt into the same wheel in the same model car in the same factory in Detroit, but it can sure feel like it. Routine, no matter how complex the work, will eventually lead to burnout.

So how do you fight burnout? Since it is caused by inflexible routine, you have to put new things into your job. Adding some new responsibilities, transferring to a new office, or associating with different co-workers may be the only change you need. Or, more dramatic measures include changing companies or even careers. Regardless of the degree of the change, change is indeed your antidote.

Emptiness

Former high achievers who became victims of burnout seem to have a few things in common. First, their priorities and interests have changed and their career no longer has a strong connection to what they care about. The passions have shifted but their activities have not. Instead of being their method of fulfillment, work has become an interference.

Also, the burned-out folks tend to have made a career out of a succession of short-term goals. Rather than look at their career over the long haul, they have satisfied themselves with more immediate goals, or worse yet, no goals whatsoever. So what's wrong with short-term goals? When they fit into an overall big picture or combined to achieve a common cause, there is absolutely nothing wrong whatsoever. In fact, short-term goals can be used as wonderful tools that provide a sense of regular achievement as well as stepping stones to your overall purpose. But without an overall cause or purpose to move toward, short-term goals only serve to make you fell shallower and without any purpose—ergo, burnout and depression. (In the words of that joyful philosopher Peggy Lee, *Is that all there is?*)

And then these former high achievers reach mid-life and mid-career. They begin to feel this lack of accomplishment in their lives and immediately turn to the source of all their previous problem solutions. They look to their work to solve the emptiness they are getting from their work! This is not unlike using "the hair of the dog" as the cure for a hangover. Obviously their work, which has caused the problem, is not going to solve it, so, they blame their company for their issues even though most companies are just not capable of identifying—much less curing—the emptiness a formerly sterling employee is feeling. The result? Either the company tolerates a depressed, low-productivity employee or the two eventually part ways. Everyone loses.

Wow. Writing all that is really depressing. So let's lighten things up and discuss solutions. The most important thing to understand is that the solution lies with you. Your company can't solve this, neither can your spouse or coworkers or boss. You can start by working to prevent the issue. You've had many years to contemplate the subject of your life's purpose and your long-term goals. Doing so will lead to actions on your part that will help cut off this seemingly inevitable drive toward mid-career blues. But if it's too late for prevention, then use the same antidote to begin curing the issue. Focus on the long term.

Identify the things most important to you and make a plan to get there. Have short-term goals that lead to long-term objectives. Make note of your abilities and interests and then see where they match. For instance, notice the areas where you are doing well at but really don't enjoy or even care. Take a different approach. Decide what it is you really care about and then get good at it. You may be doing something you're good at, but don't enjoy. Instead, find something you enjoy and then learn what it takes to get good at it.

Yes, I know this process is easy to say but hard to do. But the point is, no one can do this for you. No one can make your goals or make your plan for you. The ball is completely in your court.

But here is the kicker. The solutions to job burnout are not always found in the office. We Boomers tend to wrap up our entire selves and identity in our jobs. We think that if we are having any problems in our lives it is because of our jobs. And if the problem is with our job then the solution must also be there. Realize the solution just might be elsewhere. Do you have a need to contribute, to help others, or for variety? Look outside your office for opportunities to mentor, volunteer, or even just to have fun. Begin a second career based on interests you have that have nothing at all to do with your job. (See chapter 10 and study the new definition of retirement to get a good perspective on how these actions can fit in well with long-term goals.)

One last word on burnout and the mid-career crisis. What is the worst thing you can do about it? The worst course of action is to do nothing. If you think, *This thing will pass*, you are forever sentenced to being in this rut. The circumstances will not change on their own. You must take responsibility and you must take action. Take responsibility for change, and change will happen.

Hank's Story

For more than 25 years, Hank had focused on his career, to the exclusion of his family, hobbies, friends, or any other significant personal institution. He had steadily worked his way up the corporate ladder in the finance department of a well-known consumer products company. Hank had steadily plodded along, satisfying his boss, upper management, co-workers, and clients until one day he woke up in a depressed funk. Hank knew the problem immediately. The career he had sacrificed everything for was unsatisfying. No, that was just too soft of an expression. Hank hated his job, his career, his whole life.

Hank had hit midlife and he didn't like it. To begin curing this "illness," Hank began paying more attention to the gap between the reality of his life and the dreams he once had. Hank was determined to pounce on his one last chance for a career that could make the second half of his life fulfilling.

Two years later, Hank bought a small bait and tackle shop near Minnow Lake. (He moved his family to a small home nearby, thus saving his marriage and family, but that is another story not really within the scope of this book. But nice to know, nonetheless.) He loves his new life.

Changing careers is just one aspect to the midlife crisis. As we reach midlife, parents and friends begin to die. We begin to realize that our lives will come to an end someday and question whether we want to spend the rest of the time we have doing the same thing we've been doing. We remember all the dreams and goals we had in college and it becomes important—urgent?—to get back on track with our original plan.

Hank's story is not all that unusual. A growing number of us are looking at our forties and fifties as the right time to start fresh. It's a positive reaction to our midlife blues.

✳✳✳

A close friend recently faced his 50th birthday. It was hitting him hard, in fact it sparked a genuine midlife crisis. Fortunately, he didn't address the crisis through the common *buy-a-red-sports-car-and-run-off-to-Hawaii* gambit. Andy found a healthier release by taking long walks through the woods and doing some quality cogitating.

One day he was taking one of his walks when a truly amazing thing happened. A frog jumped right in the middle of his path, sat down, and looked him straight in the eye. And then it spoke. "Please sir, I need your help," the frog began. "I am not actually a frog, but a beautiful princess." This caught Andy's attention. "A wicked witch cast this spell on me and it will not be broken until I am kissed. If you will kiss me I will turn back into a beautiful princess and serve you the rest of my life."

"Well I'll be darned," Andy said as he reached down, picked up the frog princess, and placed her in the pocket of his jacket. Andy then leisurely continued his walk.

"Hey, what are you doing!" the frog screamed. "Weren't you listening? Kiss me. Beautiful princess. Lifetime service. Didn't you hear me?"

"Yeah, I heard you," Andy said. "But at this point in my life, I think I'd rather have a talking frog."

Chapter 3

Reentering

"The role of the woman" has changed dramatically since most Boomers left college. Because of these changes, some of the good advice for men is poor guidance for women. For instance, many Boomer women spent their early adult years caring for their family or being underemployed. At a time when Boomer men are beginning their second or third career, many women are just now able to begin their first career. In that circumstance they tend to underestimate their marketability and compete with younger workers for entry-level positions. This results in misemployment, which leads to a career that is underpaid, not challenging, and emotionally miserable.

OBSTACLES

Much as we'd like it otherwise, Boomer women still face obstacles men do not. Some of these issues are well known. Women still earn less than their male counterparts. Professional women on their way up still deal with having to prove themselves in areas in which men are simply assumed to be competent. And many women are trying to do it all—have a full rewarding career while also raising a family. (How does one do this, exactly? Actually it is quite simple. As one single mom explained to me, "Sleep is greatly overrated.")

Women CEOs are still a dramatic minority, depriving young GenX and Millennial women of badly needed mentors. And the women who have made the executive suite have to deal with labels. If a man outfoxes a business opponent, he is called "shrewd." A woman doing the same is called a "bitch."

In fact, this same labeling occurs at all levels in the workforce. I can remember receiving so many compliments every time I would take off work to attend a daughter's ball game, have a parent/teacher conference, or occasionally pick her up at school due to illness. I can't count the number of times I was complimented for being such a "good father who is involved with your kids." On the other hand, I can remember discussions about the women in the office who did the same thing. They were said to need to learn how to stop having their work interrupted by their children.

It is interesting how much depends on your gender. Sure there are other differences; for instance men, in general, are stronger than women. And this was indeed a legitimate reason for discrimination back in the days where so many jobs depended on physical strength. But most of those jobs either no longer exist or technological advances have rendered strength unnecessary.

Not too long ago there was a common thinking that women were not as smart intellectually or not as good managers as men, but all that has been dispelled; in fact it is now common wisdom that females are actually a bit superior to men in these areas.

There is also the subject of so-called women's work. While women are not restricted from any profession, there still remains a great divide between jobs for men and those for women. The Department of Labor researched the jobs in which women dominated the workforce. Notice any pattern?

Table 3.1 Industries Dominated by Women (2007)

Occupation	Percent
secretaries and administrative assistants	96.7
child care workers	94.6
hairdressers, stylists, cosmetologists	92.9
registered nurses	91.7
teacher assistants	91.5
medical assistants and other health care support	90.6
auditing clerks	90.3
maids and housekeeping services	89.2
home health aides	88.3
elementary and middle school teachers	80.9
office clerks, general	85.3
cashiers	75.6
supervisors, office managers, and admin support	73.4
customer service representatives	68.5
accountants and auditors	61.8

With the exception of the addition of women as accountants and auditors, I believe this same chart could have been published in 1970. (Part of the blame for this is that many women migrate toward jobs that have been traditionally done by women. If you seek such a path, don't be shocked if that is where you wind up.)

Now the purpose of this riff is certainly not to prove women's equality to men. I doubt anyone who disputes this equality would be reading this (or any) book. Actually, I direct my remarks at women. You know that you are fully qualified to take your place in the workforce as does just about every person who may be in the position to hire you. But here is my point. While the statistics for women are discouraging, it is your experience that matters, not group statistics. Do not be discouraged by stats that say there are few female CEOs or brain surgeons. The fact is there may be some bumpy roads between you and your dreams, but there are no roadblocks. Unless you want to be a major league baseball umpire, your dreams are there to be had.

THE BIG ISSUE FOR WOMEN

As you have just seen, there are many issues remaining that separate women from full equal opportunity in the workforce. Many books could be (and have been) written on this issue, but I want to focus on one wedge of the problem. I feel the biggest employment issue facing Boomer women today is some variation of this issue: when a woman begins a career, then marries, and quits her career to raise her family, and then—right about her husband's 45th birthday—there is a divorce, the woman is now a single mom and forced to restart her career after 20 years out of the workplace.

If you want to meet a true hero, all you need to do is open your front door and look up and down your street. Single mothers are everywhere. Single moms have to do it all. They have to be a mom and a dad, raise the children while holding down a full-time job (for which they are often paid 84 cents for what a man is paid $1 . . . but I digress).

I do a lot of work as a career counselor. I charge a respectable fee for those who can afford it. I charge nothing for people referred by Crossroads Career Network ministry and single moms. Those single moms have taught me a lot about dealing with challenges. And I've taught them a lot about dealing with the issue of getting a career after being out of the workforce. Let me share a couple of their stories.

Carol was married for 24 years to an Air Force officer. She had a brief career as an office manager but quit when she had her first child and her husband was transferred to Germany. Carol's world was upside down when her husband retired and the couple divorced. The kids were now in college, but there was not enough money in the settlement to even care for herself. She felt desperate because, having been out of the job market for a couple of decades, she felt thought she had no marketable skills. As we learned from the last chapter, this was not true. But it took a while to convince Carol of this as I did an exhaustive interview of her past activities. No surprise to me, the deeper I probed the more I learned about the amazing things Carol did during this employment gap. This new knowledge led to these accomplishment bullet points on her resume:

- Personally welcomed and oriented new military families in Germany.
- Aided these families in solving problems, such a communicating back home, budgeting, school registration, and referring to marriage counselors.
- Headed fundraising projects to help families experiencing financial difficulties; programs raised over $3,000,000 in 12 years.
- Coordinated six family moves in 20 years; two were international.

Carol obtained a part-time job as an office assistant with a quality company. Meanwhile she is now going back to school to get her accounting degree.

And then there was Ellen. Like Carol, she had been married for over 20 years to a man who owned a business. The business had done quite well, allowing Carol to stay at home and focus on her large family. But when the last one was out of the house, her husband filed for divorce, took the business, and was ordered to give her only a small temporary alimony. Carol was panicked. She needed a job and she had no skills. Or at least so she thought.

It seems that Carol did a bit more than herd the rug rats while she stayed home all those years. She also answered the business phone and sold services to clients. Carol kept the books, paid employees, and took care of tax deposits. She put together business loan applications and once initiated a complex refinancing. And, she had her hands in a few dozen other critical business needs. "Why did you think you didn't have some marketable business skills?" I asked.

"Oh, that," she answered. "He didn't pay me for any of that."

Ladies, understand this. Just like Carol and Ellen you don't have to be paid in order to have solid, documented business accomplishments. Even if you have never had a formal job, you have most definitely had experiences and accomplishments and skills that many employers would love to have in their employees.

REENTERING AFTER A DIVORCE

Looking for a job is a tough process for a Boomer under any circumstances, but it is a special challenge if you a newly divorced woman who has been out of the workforce for many years. In addition to the emotional strain you are probably still under, you may be filled with self doubts and fear of the interview process. Here are some suggestions of how to hurdle these obstacles and return to a promising career.

Learn Today's Job Search Skills

Getting a job today is a lot different than it was in 1985. Rather than learning this by trial and error, get acquainted with the new way to be hired. Reading this book is a good start; employment is one of the main themes of *The Boomers' Career Survival Guide*. But don't stop here. Many churches, schools, and community groups offer *free* classes and workshops on how to find a position in today's changed climate. Your state's Department of Employment can be a rich garden of information and connections. Do not ignore this excellent resource. Check the Sunday newspapers for a listing of community groups offering employment education and assistance.

Enlist a Support Team

If your divorce has been recent, realize that dealing with a divorce and job search at the same time is emotionally and physically exhausting. Never try to face these crises alone. If you do, you will fail miserably and take three steps back for every one you take forward. Friends and family can be indispensable, but don't hesitate to secure help from "outside" sources as well. Sometimes therapy may be in order.

Get Current

Your biggest legitimate danger is that you are no longer current in your area. New methods and techniques, new terminology and legislation, and new technology may have passed you by. Potential employers will need to be satisfied that you won't attempt to solve today's problems using 1985 solutions. So how do you deal with that? Time to hit the books. Start with the computer. Sure, you have kept up with basic programs, but how about software that has become standard in your particular field?

And, reacquaint yourself with the business world. Read the trade journals and attend any meetings of professional groups. Have lunch or coffee with former colleagues to simply talk shop. Dive back in to your profession and get current with the culture.

Deal with the Time Gap

I know that right now you think your time out of the workforce is a big problem. It is a big problem if you haven't been doing anything or if you spent it in prison. But if the time was spent raising a family, it really isn't a gap. Be prepared to explain it? Yes. Agonize over it? Nope.

Employers beyond their Cro-Magnon years understand the importance of family and the choices parents make. A simple "I was at home with my children" will suffice during the interview process. Proceed to explain the skills you have and the updating you have done to prepare yourself for the position you are discussing. Focus on the skills you have rather than justifying gaps taken for the sake of your family.

Network

This book thoroughly discusses the concept of networking and how it will almost certainly be the source of your next job. So I won't jump ahead with the details of networking right now, but I do want to emphasize the necessity of using this tool. Networking is the tool for accomplishing just about anything in business today—not only in getting a job, but in accomplishing projects and creating quality work. So, right from the start, get comfortable with meeting people and establishing strong working relationships.

Meet people through mutual friends and contacts and referrals. Does this make you uncomfortable? Is it outside your normal method of operation? Relax. As you'll see, it is so much easier than you think it is. Others are just as eager to meet you and build business friendships. Everybody wins.

Reach for Your Dreams, but Be Realistic

Perhaps you've decided that you want a salary of $50,000. Then you are offered a job paying $40,000. You wanted a job that had bankers hours, but the one you have been offered (at a bank no less) requires that you work until 7:00 P.M. and every other Saturday. Think a bit before you reject the offer. How will you feel if you turn it down and then your job search extends several more months?

Now my point is not that you should take any job offered or that your sights are set too high. What I am saying is that you must do your research and decide what is really important to you versus what are your nice-to-haves. There are jobs out there for you, but not an endless supply that you can tweak until they reflect perfection.

Think out of the Box

For instance, consider working for a company part-time. That will get you inside the company and give you a chance to look around. You can learn new skills on their dime. And, perhaps the best part, expand into a full-time position later. As discussed later, it's much easier to get a quality job in a company once you are inside that company.

Another similar strategy is to work on a special project as an independent contractor. Again, you will get a chance to experience the company's culture while they get a chance to interact with you and learn the quality of your work. Here's the point. There are a lot of ways to joint the workforce other than with a traditional full-time employment. Be creative in your approach.

Watch the Attitude

As tough as it may be, be sure to separate the personal from the professional when interviewing. Your feelings of anger and insecurity are understandable, but the fact remains that potential employers really don't want to hear about how unfair life has treated you lately. Instead, focus on impressing the potential employer by emphasizing the contributions you can make to the future success of the organization.

It's also a turnoff to show any sense of financial desperation. Instead of focusing on the negative reasons as to why you're returning to work, tell the positive. "After a few years at home devoted to my family, I'm now ready to recommit myself to my career."

✳✳✳

Returning to the job market can be tough. But with some learning, professionalism, hard work, and a little help from a lot of friends, you will start on a new career path. Any human resource manager will tell you how hard it is to find talented employees with a strong, positive work ethic. You have a lot to give, so get out there and prove it.

Chapter 4

Rebounding

If at first you don't succeed, try, try again. And then give up. No sense in being a damned fool about it.

—Mark Twain

Remember the Ron Howard movie *Apollo 13*? The scientists and engineers on the ground were scurrying like windmills in a tornado to devise a miracle solution that could save the crippled spacecraft. Gene Kranz, the director of mission control, barked each person's assignments and then dramatically added, "Failure is not an option!"

Well, actually failure is always an option. And sometimes it's the smart option. How we succeed is often determined by how we fail. It's not the failure itself, it is how we react to it and what we learn from it. It could be said that failure is simply a natural step on the way to success. Just because you have failed many times does not mean you are a failure. Remember Thomas Edison's take on the subject? He tried 9,000 methods to make a lightbulb before he finally found one that worked. Did he see that as 9,000 failures? Not at all. He just considered that he succeeded in finding 9,000 ways that a lightbulb would not work.

I can do a lot of things well, but sales is not one of them. It's not because I can't be convincing, because that I can do. It is because I can't stand rejection. Now, once I get in front of the client I am actually pretty good. When I was much younger I held a sales position. My manager called me in his office one day to make a point. "Ken, you have the lowest sales dollar total in the district. On the other hand, you hold the district record for closings— you close two out of every three sales. Ken, what you need is more *threes*." That fear of rejection had developed a call reluctance that resulted in very few sales appointments, which ended my attempt at a sales career.

I really should have paid more attention to some of the techniques successful salespeople use to overcome call reluctance. One is quite logical. A top sales executive determined that he averaged one sale for every nine calls he made. While I would hear that and just notice that nine calls equaled eight no's, he thought of each rejection differently. Upon hearing his sixth no, this man would think, "Good to get that out of the way. I only need to make three more calls to get a sale."

Another top performer had the same call/sale ratio but viewed the statistics differently. He averaged $450 commission on each sale. So, whether he made a sale or not, he considered every phone call to be worth $50. I admire and highly respect the way these men think. These are healthy and productive ways to view failure. Think of each failure as a valuable step in progress toward your goals.

BENEFITS OF FAILURE

I'll bet you are thinking, *Wow, Ken, you are going a little overboard with your optimism.* I'll accept the criticism, but just hang in with me on this. Failure provides countless benefits to your career as long as you recognize their potential and capture those benefits for yourself. Look at these:

Failure Gives Us Experience. We tend to become a little bit smarter and a bit more aware each time we hit a brick wall. We learn new tricks of the trade, new routes to the goal, or new ways to prepare for the next event. We know what to do next time. Actually, through the process of failure, we may have actually found a better route. But what if we had luckily breezed through on our first venture? We would think that there was nothing to it and would be grossly unprepared in the future. A future of constantly bashing our head into brick walls.

Failure Encourages Innovation. We look for new methods, pathways, and tools when confronted with failure. And sometimes, like Edison, this search leads to new innovations.

Failure Drives Learning. If you don't fail, you aren't learning and you aren't even living. With failure you grow as a person, learning about your own strengths and weaknesses. You learn a lot about your friends and acquaintances, finding out quickly who is loyal and who flies away under adversity. These are business lessons you can't learn in school.

Failure Can Push You in a New Direction. Sometimes failure is God's way of saying, "You ain't supposed to be doing that." Failure will often push you in a better direction. Early failure is so much better than that which comes after years of struggle. Early failure lets you know if you are not cut out for that business or perhaps that the time is not right. Subtle issues are often the cause of failure; if it comes early enough you may be able to adapt, make a few changes, and then flourish.

Failure Builds Character. I know what you are thinking. If failure builds character then I must be the biggest character in the state! We learn a lot about ourselves when we stumble. We can choose to quit or choose to brush ourselves off and keep plugging. Either way, our inner self is shaped a little bit more each time we face the decision.

HOW FAILURE BREEDS SUCCESS

As we consider the benefits of failure (now there is a phrase you just don't hear every day), it might be good to glance at how one corporation views company failures. Just like people, companies also fear failure. In fact most companies recoil at the thought of a program failing. While few companies cover up their hiccups, neither do they go out of the way to publicize their failures outright.

An argument could be made that Coca-Cola is the most successful company in the world. Despite this, Coke is well known for its colossal failures. Remember New Coke? How about something more recent—ever heard of Choglit or OK Soda or Surge? This incredibly successful company has certainly had its share of embarrassing failures.

Given Coke's conservative reputation, it would seem that the last thing the CEO would want to discuss is a failure. And if he did, he certainly wouldn't choose to discuss it in front of his stockholders. Yet that is exactly what CEO Neville Isdell did. He told the gathering, "You will see some failures. As we take more risks, this is something we must accept as part of the regeneration process" (McGregor 2006).

Isdell wants Coke to take bigger risks, but the only way to do that would be for the company, its management, and its stockholders to accept a culture of risks. Isdell made it clear that he will tolerate the failures that are an inevitable by-product of innovation.

That is a healthy view of failure by a corporation and a healthy view for an individual to take. Failures that are a by-product of reasonable risks are learning and growth opportunities.

IS IT REALLY A FAILURE?

Christopher Columbus set out to discover a new trade route to India. He failed. We could compile a long list of examples of people and companies creating brilliant successes on the back of initially embarrassing failures. Here is one of my favorites.

Dr. Spence Silver was a Master Tape Engineer at 3M. His search for a strong new adhesive resulted in the creation of a weak and flabby glue. His months of work ended in a miserable failure. But actually, due to the culture of 3M, the experiment did not end.

In most companies Dr. Spence would have swept the results under the rug and fought to save his career. But it didn't work that way at 3M. Instead of fleeing, he shared his "discovery" with his coworkers, including Allen Fry. A few weeks after this conversation, Mr. Fry was having trouble while singing in his church choir. Pieces of paper that he had stuck in the hymnal to mark songs kept falling out. He used some of Dr. Spencer's glue and, before you could say *stick 'em up!* the Post-It note was invented. A colossal failure, a brilliant success.

HMM, TIME TO COGITATE

All successful people were once failures. All of them. Here is the difference between people who end up with success and those who seem to be mired in it forever. When successful people fail, they pick themselves up, brush themselves off and try again from a slightly different angle.

Abraham Lincoln, received no more than five years of formal education throughout his lifetime. He was a pretty good lawyer but was a failure as a politician. Out of 14 races, Abe only won 3. He was elected once to Congress and two terms as president of the United States. Historians, however, tend to rank him as America's greatest president.

Michael Jordan is the greatest basketball player of all time. Before his junior year in college Jordan was a rather mediocre player. In fact he was cut from his high school basketball team because of his "lack of skill."

Walt Disney started his first business from his home garage and soon went bankrupt. During his press conference, a newspaper editor ridiculed Walt Disney because he had no good ideas in film production.

Henry Ford's first two automobile companies failed. Henry examined the causes of those failures and tried again. He began the Ford Motor Company, where he implemented the assembly line, began paying workers living wages, and offered low prices to his customers. This combination revolutionized manufacturing in the world.

Albert Einstein, failing to get a teaching job at his alma mater, instead landed a job at the patent office. And it was there that, rather than playing solitaire on his computer, Einstein sat around thinking. He did such a good job thinking that he came up with the concept of space-time. Eventually he was able to take a full-time job as a thinker and was eventually recognized as the most brilliant thinker of the 20th century.

Lisa Kudrow was fired by the producers of *Frasier,* who, after the initial pilot episode, didn't think she was a good "Ros." So she landed the part of Phoebe on a new show, *Friends*.

Stephen King received 30 rejections and the author threw his new novel in the trash. Luckily his wife fished it out again and encouraged him to resubmit it. The book was *Carrie*, and it went on to be a huge success both in the bookstores as well as the movies.

These examples are just a very few of those I could have listed. What about you? If you fit the definition of "successful," I'll bet you could create a pretty impressive list of your own. How many examples can you come up with where an absolute disaster forced you into a wonderful situation? How many of you were in absolutely miserable jobs, were laid off in a corporate downsizing, and then landed in a wonderful situation in the next job? On the other hand, there are millions of people who held "tolerable" jobs and did not get laid off. And then, since they were never forced to look elsewhere, they never stumbled into that position that brought them great satisfaction and significant discoveries.

Failure sometimes isn't.

YOUR ACCOMPLISHMENTS

Q: When you apply for a mortgage, what is the only thing a lender really wants to know?
A: Will you pay the money back?
Q: What is the best thing the bank can look at to determine the answer to this?
A: Your credit rating.

Banks know that the best way to determine future actions is to look at past behavior. Your credit rating gives the lender a pretty good idea of whether or not you will make timely payments on their loan.

It works the same way with employers. What are they most interested in knowing about you? How good a job you will do for them. And what is the best way for them to predict the future quality of your work? By looking at what you have done in the past. Using this train of thought, let's spend some time making it easy for the employer to determine your future actions. Let's make a list that will have multiple uses for you as you plan then rest of your career.

Not Just a Bunch of Theory

So why are we having this long discussion about accomplishments? We are focusing on this because so much of this book makes use of this knowledge and the exercise soon to follow. Look at four primary uses of this:

Your resume. The focal point of the resume you will develop is in your accomplishments. Remember that past behavior indicates future actions. By focusing on your accomplishments, your resume will announce that you are a person with a future.

The job interview. As you learned in chapter 2, job interviews have changed quite a bit in the last 20 years. Instead of a dry Q&A session, interviews have become more like conversations that include stories and examples. It's no longer good enough to declare that you are a "people person"; now you need to give several examples of how you have used your people skills to achieve success. Your accomplishments will serve as a ready reserve of examples for all of your many positive traits.

Your sweet spot. And as you will see in the next chapter, you must find your "sweet spot" if you expect to align yourself with the career you are best suited for. Looking for patterns in your accomplishments will highlight your skills, interests, and strengths.

Your self-image. There is yet another benefit to studying your accomplishments, and this one might be the most important. As you collect these accomplishments, you will gain a great deal of self-confidence. You will appreciate what you have done and understand that you do have a lot to offer an employer.

But I Haven't Really Done Anything

I often hear that remark from the people I coach. In fact I've heard it so many times that I have now learned how to suppress the urge to run from the building screaming as if my hair was on fire. Here is the bottom line on thinking you have no accomplishments. If you define accomplishment as winning a Nobel Prize or an Olympic medal, or equate it with being president of Brazil or accumulating a billion dollars, then OK, I'll agree that you probably haven't accomplished much. But if you breathe in oxygen and exhale CO_2, I'm betting we can easily find over a few dozen significant accomplishments in your life. You don't agree? Here is why you disagree— you take your accomplishments for granted. Here is my favorite example.

I was volunteering at a career ministry several years ago and was helping Ray with his resume. Ray was a 50-year-old truck driver, a nice but terribly humble man. I used the adverb "terribly" to define "humble" because Ray answered all my appeals by saying, "Ken, I'm just a truck driver. I've never really accomplished anything." (Ray is the type of guy who begins diary entries, *Dear Diary, Sorry to bother you again . . .*) I was tiring of his low self-esteem and suggested we take a break. As we sipped on some coffee, Ray casually mentioned, "You know, Ken, I've driven over a million miles in my career. Never had an accident, never even gotten a ticket."

I leaped out of my chair, surprising Ray so much that he spit out some coffee. "Ray! Do you have any idea what you just said?" I asked. Ray apparently thought he was in trouble, because his eyes were the size of ping-pong balls. I continued. "A lot of trucking managers will be looking at your resume right after they've signed a huge check to their insurance company."

Ray eventually pounced on what I had in mind and we came up with several other good accomplishments, including a couple dealing with his attendance and training abilities. Follow-up: Ray found a job within two weeks, picking from several fine offers. In fact, he received an offer from every company he applied to. (Legal disclaimer: Results are not guaranteed. Your results may vary.)

Here is my point. You have many accomplishments in your life that would not only impress a future employer but will also impress you. The reason we don't readily recognize these accomplishments is that we tend to take our strengths for granted. These actions come naturally and easily for you, so you assume everyone has them. Trust me on this—they don't.

Some Examples

OK, if an accomplishment does not have to be winning a Pulitzer or being awarded the Medal of Honor, what defines what an accomplishment looks like? Here is a random list of actions that in my book are definitely accomplishments:

- Employee of the Month, 7 out of 12 months in 2006.
- Speak, read, and write Spanish at an intermediate level.
- Created an in-store display that increased product sales 40%. The rest of the stores in the district duplicated both the display as well as the sales increase.
- Raised three amazing kids as a single parent after spouse passed away.
- Net profit before taxes has always beaten budget.
- Served on company committee reviewing possible cost savings.
- Have exceeded sales quota every quarter for last seven years.
- Completed training program, scoring in top 10% of the company.
- Wrote a manual showing how to properly handle customer complaints now used throughout the company.
- In the last eight years, never missed a day of work, despite raising three young children.

- Elected vice chair of local political action committee.
- Supervised construction of eight stores in 2008. All opened ahead of schedule and under budget.
- Successfully led effort to convince the city council to deny zoning for a huge retail center to be built in a quiet family neighborhood.
- As a customer complaint manager for huge restaurant chain, personally handled over 6,000 complaints last year with a 96.7% retention rate.

Business accomplishments do not have to be performed at a business. You do not have to be paid for something for it to indicate accomplishment, skills, or character. Examples?

- Coordinated PTA fundraising auction netting over $60,000.
- Taught family finance class at church for three years.
- As Scoutmaster for Troop 32, saw 19 scouts complete a special program of my design and receive their Eagle ranking.
- Volunteered to help 19 poor families fill out their income tax returns.
- Counseled victims of domestic violence, including helping them navigate the legal system.
- Through a self-designed physical development program, worked my way from couch potato to running a 5K within a year.
- Completely redecorated my home drawing favorable reviews from professional interior decorators.

Homework? I Don't Want No Stinkin' Homework!

I mentioned earlier what a powerful tool a list of accomplishments can be. It is the highlight of your resume. It is what separates you from the rest of the pack at an interview. The list will help point you towards your sweet spot and save you from a career choice that could leave you miserable. And, perhaps most important, the list will build your self-confidence as you realize just how unique and useful you really are. Considering the impact it will have on your life, making the list is worth missing a few reruns of *Star Trek* or *Gunsmoke*.

So here is the assignment. Make a list of 100 accomplishments you have had in your life. (Yes, I said 100.) Since not all these accomplishments will be used for business or career-related purposes, feel free to include items that are strictly personal. (Such as learning how to ride a bike or running a marathon or baking your first cake.) If it was an accomplishment for you, then it was an accomplishment. Put it on the list. Here are some tips on how to do this more effectively.

- Do not even try to list these in one sitting. It won't happen. Instead, break it up into several sessions over a two-week period. Sessions should never last more than 15 minutes.

- Always carry a stack of index cards. Then you can knock off a few while you are waiting at the doctor's office, having a cup of coffee, or riding on an airplane. Your best inspiration is rarely planned; it hits you while you are watching TV, driving, or chatting with friends. The index cards will help you remember these inspirations.

- Ask your spouse and close friends for suggestions. Remember we often take our amazing skills for granted. Betcha you discover some things about yourself that you had no idea.

- And—get out of the box! In fact that is the primary reason I want you to list so many. Listing 100 accomplishments forces you to get unconventional and explore your whole life.

Once you have your 100 selected, actually type out the list. Don't worry about format or length right now. You can wordsmith the items you pick for your resume when you actually write your resume. (Remember that the list is there for many reasons other than your resume.) But do group the items by their commonality. Leadership, skills, compassion, energy, whatever. Doing this helps make certain things jump out, often pointing you to an understanding what things you enjoy and excel at.

Go ahead and invest the time. We'll make heavy use of this list in the next few chapters. It'll be a great aid in guiding your future choices.

THE FAT LADY DOESN'T SING FOR A WHILE YET

I am going to be quite heavy-handed for the next few pages and using a sledgehammer to make my point. Because of this, I'll not try to subtly sneak in my point, I'll just go ahead and directly tell you right now. When you hit midlife, you can't just take what you have done thus far and double it in order to project your life's contribution. The old cliché "Life begins at 40" is really not off the mark by much. Take a look at these people and remember, these are just *some* of the *famous* ones. Imagine the length of this section if I included all the folks who aren't famous.

Neil Armstrong

In the year 2525 (*"if man is still alive . . ."*) not much will be remembered about the 20th century. The history books may include Franklin Roosevelt and World War II, but if so it will probably be, by then, little more than a footnote. On the other hand, there is one name and one event that will most certainly be highlighted in the history books forever—Neil Armstrong and the moon landing. So the man that will always be remembered for taking those first steps was (for an astronaut) an aged 40 years old.

Grandma Moses

Grandma Moses was a hard-working farmer until her retirement at 76. Frustrated by painful arthritis, she stopped her embroidery and picked up a paintbrush. She *then* had a 25-year career as America's greatest folk artist.

Colonel Harland Sanders

After a rather modest career in owning restaurants, Colonel Sanders founded the KFC chain at the age of 65. It really didn't hit its full stride until he was in his late seventies.

Ray Kroc

Ray was a traveling milk-shake mixer salesman when he was 52. That's hardly anyone's ideal job and not much of a career. Then there was the day he bought out the McDonald brothers, and the rest is history.

Sam Walton

Sam's first retail store was snatched from him by his landlord's son. Apparently his landlord noticed how much Sam's location was making so he refused to renew Sam's lease. He then turned the spot over to his own son and Sam had to look elsewhere. At first Sam was depressed but then he got busy. Yada, yada, yada, and then Sam built the world's largest retail chain as well as the largest family fortune in the history of the world. (Today, the title of the world's biggest company bounces between Walmart and Exxon-Mobil.) This all *began* when Sam Walton was 44 years old.

Ronald Reagan

This washed-up B-movie actor (you may recall that he often got second billing to a chimpanzee) was 53 when he ran for his first political office.

General George Patton

"Old Blood and Guts" was 60 when he took over command of the 2nd Armored Division, and all of his noted work came after that. Before that his superiors considered him nothing but a loud mouth pain in the rear. After that point he was considered a military genius who also happened to be a loud mouth pain in the rear.

Moses

Moses was a wanted fugitive who didn't find a real calling in life until he was 80. It was then that he led the Jewish people out of slavery in Egypt and on to the Promised Land.

Lt. Col. Dwight D. Eisenhower

Ike was 50 years old and considering retiring from the Army in early 1940. He decided to hang in a bit longer when he was promoted to full bird colonel and appointed chief of staff for the Third Infantry Division. He held several staff positions and did a good enough job that he was named as a brevet brigadier general just before the bombing of Pearl Harbor. Although his administrative abilities had been noticed, on the eve of the U.S. entry into World War II he had never held an active command and was far from being considered a potential commander of major operations. Yet by the end of the greatest war every fought, Ike was the highest ranking general in the world and considered the key force for allied victory. (Later it was rumored that Ike spent eight years in a government job in Washington; history now records him as the fifth greatest president of the United States.)

✳✳✳

This chapter has spoken about struggles, late starts, and outright failures; normally not considered fun or happy conversations. Yet under some circumstances these things can have an unexpected benefit. I've had the fortune of knowing and chatting with many successful people. You would recognize the names of some of the people I've talked with, especially the entertainers and political leaders. Others you wouldn't know offhand— doctors, teachers, religious leaders, firefighters, and so forth. But regardless of their fame, they are all tremendously successful people.

I enjoy probing the lives of these wonderful people. And whenever possible I ask a question that always fascinates me. "What was your biggest career failure?" The neat thing about this lifetime experiment is that every person—and I mean every single one—had the same immediate reaction. Before answering my question a smile would wind across their face. It was as if these highly successful men and women fondly remembered their weakest moment. They all seemed to realize that they would never have achieved unless they had experienced failure, hard times, and adversity.

Count your blessing the next time you travel over a rough road. There are things to be learned, opportunities to uncover, and character to be built.

REFERENCE

McGregor, Jena. 2006. How failure breeds success. *Business Weekly,* July 10. http://www.businessweek.com/magazine/content/06_28/b3992001. htm?campaign_id=nws_insdr_jul1&link_position=link1.

Part II

Charting Your Path

If you don't know where you are going, how will you know when you get there?

—Yogi Berra (perhaps)

Jack was driving to a critical job interview. All he had to do was complete this one final meeting with the CEO and the dream job was his.

Unfortunately he was running late and could not find a parking space. Over and over he circled the block and found nothing. Sweat rolled down his forehead as the clocked ticked off the minutes until he was late and his dreams would fly right out the window. He looked to the heavens and dramatically implored, "Please God! I need this job! If you will give me a parking place, I promise to be on the front pew every Sunday. I'll stop drinking and stop cursing. *Please!*"

And then a miracle occurred. As he turned the corner, a parking place opened up right in front of the building's entrance. Jack's eyes lit up as he looked heavenward and said, "Oh, never mind God. I found one."

While we like to think we are in full control and need no one's help, deep down we know that isn't really the case. Still, we do want to be in charge of our lives as much as we can. This is especially true with our careers. By now we realize that we do need to decide where to spend the rest of our careers and need a little help in mapping out how to get there. Here are four directions that your career can take and a little assistance for you to get there.

Chapter 5

Right Job, Right Company: Strategies

I know God will not give me any burdens I cannot handle, but sometimes I wish God did not think so highly of me.

—Mother Teresa

You enjoy your job and want to stay with your current company. But you look around and see younger workers being hired, your role diminishing, and you have lost the golden boy image you once relished. How can you stay where you are until the day you decide to retire? Here are some ways you can continue with the situation you have enjoyed and want to continue to enjoy for a while yet.

STRATEGIES FOR AVOIDING THE LAYOFFS

Perhaps the best strategy for staying with your present company is to simply not lose your job. (We'll call this the "default strategy.") In the previous generation and at the early years of Boomers this was such an obvious course of action. Keep your nose clean, don't make waves, produce your quota, move from blue collar to white collar; these were the ways to hold on to your job for a lifetime. But the concept of lifetime employment no longer exists, not even in union shops, the police department, or the priesthood. This has evolved from being a passive strategy to one that requires you to be quite active and alert.

Layoffs are rather commonplace even during the best of economic times. Stockholders place tremendous pressure on company management to produce ever-increasing quarterly profits. While it is difficult to drive income by coming up with a new product or service every three months, cutting expenses only requires an eraser. Some money can be shaved by taking a second look at office supplies and facility cleanliness, but there is one surefire way to make a massive notable impact—lay off a chunk of the workforce. And nothing gets the shareholders' tails wagging like laying off some white-collar workers.

A little cynical on my part, perhaps, but I am repulsed by unnecessarily taking away a person's livelihood just so you can show a temporary three-cent rise in the company's stock price. Employment is a sacred trust that should never be manipulated like paperclips, fuel reserves, or the hamburger inventory. To handle people—human beings—like this is unconscionable. Those that do lose all their moral integrity and any claim to leadership. But I digress.

Of course, during bad economic times employees are an obvious target for saving money. You cannot fault management's decision in this case; the company's first responsibility is to assure its survival. In fact, many jobs are often saved by eliminating others. Many of you are looking over your shoulder right now as you experience a great economic downturn. A 2009 online poll shows that most people fear the worst. It revealed that three out of four people believed their organization was likely to issue layoffs in the next 12 months. In addition, one in three people believe their job is at risk *today*.

The poor economy merged with such widespread fears should certainly result in a lot of people taking action to protect their jobs, don't you think? As it turns out, people are doing very little to secure their jobs in this weak economy. According to the survey, more that 75 percent admit they have done nothing to avoid this destiny.

Now I'm not dissing any of you. I'll assume that you simply have no idea how to avoid this fate and so you have bought this book to better your odds. (Thanks for showing this confidence in me, by the way. I appreciate it.) So let's do just that, let's improve your odds for staying with your current company. And the first step to avoiding the layoff is knowing that one is coming.

Knowing a Layoff Is Coming

At least when you are fired for poor performance you can see it coming, but usually when you are downsized (read lose your job through no fault of your own) it's hard to see the bullet. Of course when the economy is in turmoil, we all are subject to the news. But, as we previously discussed, the possibility is still there even when the economy is all rosy. Here are some things to look for that may indicate that your company is considering a layoff.

- Your company's performance is off: earnings are declining, sales are down, or market share is falling. This is especially dangerous if this has occurred for two or more quarters and a trend has been established.

- Other companies in your same industry are laying off workers. Even more telling . . . other branches of your company downsize their operations.

- There is a lot of activity around the human resource director's office. Executives are scurrying in and out; meetings are all conducted with the door closed.

- Top executives leave the company in clusters. Press releases use the phrase "for a better opportunity" or says she is retiring (and she's only 47).

- Open positions are not filled or a hiring freeze is declared. Those positions left empty are consolidated—one person hired to do three jobs.

- Executives are hired from outside the company, and they bring their own people with them.

- Training programs are reduced or eliminated. Corporate trainers are reassigned to operational positions. Always beware when a company stops investing in its people.

Here is the best way to find out if a layoff is imminent. Ask. Drop in unannounced to see either your boss or (better yet) your boss's boss. Ask her directly. One of two things will happen. She will either give you a straight answer or she will lie to you. It's so easy to tell if she is lying because bosses are lousy at lying to subordinates. Because they feel guilty, you will have no trouble reading her reaction to your question.

So, let's assume you have figured out that a layoff is in the works. Time to roll over and accept the news as final? Well, of course not. There are strategies for positioning yourself out of the line of fire.

First of All, Improve Your Performance. Layoffs are rarely arbitrary. They are often used to cull out the team and are used as way to painlessly eliminate the poorer performers. Pull out your last appraisal and make sure you have corrected any deficiencies. Better yet, drop by to see your boss and ask her for three things that she would like to see you improve. Quite often showing an attitude of wanting to improve carries the same weight as the improvement itself.

Next, Ask Your Boss for More Responsibility. Yes, this also helps improve your image, but actually this will cut to the core of protecting you in a layoff. The biggest goal of a layoff is to increase efficiency. The work still remains when workers are laid off. This conversation gives you the opportunity to show your boss that you can handle more workload, making you quite valuable if you survive the massacre.

Consider Asking for a Transfer. What's the top consideration in determining who goes and who stays? For many companies it is seniority. Nothing you can do about that? Actually, there may be. Most layoffs are done within the workgroup. (Otherwise the company would run the risk of losing the entire marketing department while not touching anyone in accounting. Or Nashville would be wiped out while Boise would survive intact.) If you rank low in seniority in your workgroup or branch location, ask to be transferred to one in which you rank higher. Actually, it's kinda nice in Boise.

Join the Untouchables. Layoffs rarely occur evenly across every department. Transfer to a department or branch that will not be affected by the layoffs. How can you see into the future? Look for a business unit that is actually hiring. The company wouldn't allow this if the layoffs were going to affect them. The department head knows his division is safe and now so do you.

Be Happy and Wave the Company Flag. Layoffs are not just the time to get rid of borderline performers, it is also an opportunity for your boss to get rid of those with a bad attitude. When told to chose the workers who are to go, you can't blame the boss for picking those who are disloyal or unsupportive. There is no better time to get on your boss's good side. I'm not advocating brown-nosing, well not exactly. But you should make it quite obvious that you love the company, enjoy your job, and absolutely adore your boss.

Layoffs are survivable, if you take the proper actions quickly. Better yet, it's not a bad idea to always approach your job as if a layoff is possible. Constantly improving your performance, asking for more responsibility, and demonstrating a great attitude will only help your career regardless of the company's economic situation.

MAKING YOUR BOSS CONTENT WITH YOU

This section is not about manipulation. We're not learning how to overpower a weak superior or to make the boss tremble at the sounds of your footsteps. Besides the fact that doing so would lead to a miserable relationship with your boss, it just wouldn't work anyway. What this section is trying to promote is a healthy relationship in which you understand the boss's needs and he understands your value to the organization. This relationship will certainly solidify your standing with the company and promote your ability to stay in the organization.

A Very Good Place to Start

Let's start at the very beginning. Let's talk basics. Before all else, before building a deep relationship, before breeding any sense of awe, before you attempt to win the employee of the year plaque, establish the basics in the relationship with your boss. These are:

Integrity. Take a stand. Even if your boss disagrees, be willing to defend your beliefs strongly. (Behind a closed door, of course.) Honesty must be assumed.

Knowledge. Your boss needs you to be the expert in your assigned area. You need to be counted on to solve problems rather than just telling him about them.

Credibility. Do what you say you're going to. Your word must be gospel.

Professionalism. Look and act like a person your boss would be proud to take to a meeting of the board of directors.

Caring. Show that you care about your boss, his career, and his opinions.

Speak the Same Language

Does this happen to you? You present a report on a project you have been working on and your boss just quietly nods. Or maybe you discuss some activities you have been engaged in and he looks confused. If this is a common occurrence, the problem you have is that you and your boss are not on the same page.

Here is a little exercise that will not only diagnose this issue but will also cure it. Though I warn you, the exercise may be a bit painful for both of you. Both you and your boss make separate lists of your job duties, expectations, and current priorities. Compare lists. You will both be shocked.

Now between you and me, we'll blame this disjoint in communication on your boss; however, between you and your boss just say that you are disappointed to be so far off track. Arrange another discussion to get you aligned with your boss's roadmap. This little exercise, repeated every year or so, will go a long way in keeping a great relationship with your boss as well as driving an impressive performance review.

Hold on to Your Monkey

Don't just bring your boss problems, bring solutions. Problems follow a definite route. There is a gap between an objective and the result. There are several options to close the gap. One needs to be chosen and resources assigned.

Yes, it is your responsibility to notify the boss whenever you are aware of a hiccup in the system, but you must go beyond that. Take the process all the way through, write it up, and tell him, "Here is the way I propose to handle it."

Now you might already know all this. Just make sure you actually do it this way. Because GenX's Jennifer and Christopher grew up in the business world thoroughly understanding this part of problem solving.

Learn Boss-speak

I have mellowed over the years. Early on, when I was in my mid-twenties running some fast-food chains, if I didn't like something I would yell, "This sucks. You need to get things in line and get it done by yesterday!" A bit later in my career I would respond to the same situation by quietly pulling the supervisor aside and telling him, "I'm disappointed. Let's see what can be done about this, OK?" Two different statements, both meaning the same thing. Understand that many phrases can mean different, sometimes even opposite, things depending on whose mouth it is coming out of. Learn exactly what your boss means when he says, "If you have time . . ." or "As soon as you can . . ." or "Have you considered . . ."

Surprise, Surprise, Surprise!

Bosses are like the stock market; they hate surprises. Other than on his birthday, never surprise your boss. Surprising your boss, even with good news, causes him to forever after be looking over his shoulder at you. He will be worried about what you are really up to as well as identify you as unreliable. That's a lousy reputation to have.

Bad news ages poorly; always tell your boss at the earliest indication. Don't become the worrisome twit with a black cloud always hanging over your head, but if it looks like you are not going to make your sales quota or blow some expense item, don't let his first notification be when he picks up the quarterly P&L.

I'm sure you have heard the strategy of "Around here it's easier to get forgiveness than to get permission." Baloney. Bosses hate forgiving. If you want to take on a project, get permission first. If the boss says no, he probably knows something you don't. Get his input to assure that your efforts are directed toward the big picture, not just the wedge you are aware of.

While this insight is important for employees of all generations, it is especially important to Boomers who have a new boss or one that is younger. They often perceive you as a potential threat (because of your experience) and any surprises—good or bad—tend to show them up or make them look bad. Demonstrate your support by keeping them fully in the loop.

Mature Your Relationship

The relationship with your boss will reach new heights if you develop it beyond simply just comfortable. The ideal relationship comes when your boss sees you as a kindred spirit, a team member who shares many business brain cells, a Watson to his Sherlock. When the relationship hits this level, you will find that your boss does more than just give you good scores on your performance review. He will actually look after your interests when times are good while protecting you when times are turbulent.

The most important way to begin the evolution is to let him know you are competent, knowledgeable beyond your assigned area, and absolutely trustworthy. But then you need to take it another step. Cultivate an interest in something that also interests the boss. A good example would be to learn how to play golf if your boss likes to talk business while playing golf. If you and your boss have the same political beliefs, perhaps you can go to party events with him. (I know, possible dangers here.) And if the boss is a huge fan of the Atlanta Braves (and who isn't?) arrange to regularly attend games together—even if you live in Boston. If attending the games or joining the party seems a bit much, at least keep up with the same interests. Learn about the WBA or the NRA or the CIA or whatever acronym fits just so you can have some conversation with him beyond business.

Now a fine line exists between establishing a well-rounded business relationship and becoming buddies, which is something to avoid. I'm not sure how to identify that line, but to borrow the logic of Supreme Court Justice Potter Stewart when defining pornography, *I'll know it when I see it.* And so will you.

SURVIVING A YOUNGER BOSS

A startling moment occurred in my life at 10:02 P.M. on November 4, 2008. At that moment I realized that my doctor was younger than me. My attorney was younger than me. The guy I was about to go into business with was nine years younger than me (and he was to be the *senior* partner.) And now, the president of the United States—the *president* for Pete's sake—was younger than me. This was a hard moment to accept.

Perhaps what made it so tough to deal with was the fact that I was a wonder boy growing up. I was always the youngest at whatever I did. My subordinates were always much older and I learned to accept the world on those terms.

Another vivid memory. At the age of 24 I was a regional director for a fledgling restaurant chain. There were five supervisors reporting to me; the youngest was 30, the oldest 48. Sales had been soft and upper management decided to cut expenses, including the cost of one supervisor. I was to pick the supervisor. No matter how I analyzed it (the least effective person was also lowest in seniority), the choice had to be Brady, the 48-year-old.

I gave him the news and he did not take it well. An hour later, Brady's wife called me. In fact, she called me every name in the book. She ended her eloquent soliloquy with this message, "Ken, I like you. You're a nice young fellow. I just hope that when you are 48 someone half your age doesn't take away your family's livelihood."

So what is the point of this mini-biography? It is this: If you have a younger boss, cut him some slack. It's not his fault that you are older than he is.

Now that's a long route to make the point, but it is a necessary route. Much of the tension in these types of couplings is caused by the older worker's oversensitivity to the situation. The younger boss doesn't have the life experiences to deal with your middle-aged issues and mountains. Often his efforts to do so get mangled and misinterpreted, leading to further frustration for both of you. Cut him some slack.

Let's face it. Older workers can be difficult to manage. Young supervisors have confided that older workers do not respect them and their opinions are dismissed. They often hear responses such as, "Let me tell you how we have always done things around here," and, "Well, maybe that's what they taught you in college but . . ." We Boomers can be set in our ways, resistant to change, and obnoxious know-it-alls. And so when they are choosing someone to promote or hire, younger bosses often feel more comfortable with younger people who are more respectful. This preference is technically age discrimination. I use the word "technically" only because such a preference violates the *letter* of the law. Frankly, I do not believe it violates the spirit of the law. We Boomers are often to blame for the evils done against us—we sometimes create situations that make discrimination look like a totally reasonable response.

Now that little discussion probably makes many of you angry. After all, I am a Boomer writing a book to help Boomers. You're assuming I came to praise Boomers, not bury them. Consider the proceeding as tough love. We must understand that the single biggest problem with younger bosses lies with the older workers' attitude toward them. Cut them some slack.

Now that that is out of the way, let's look at some other methods for bringing peace to the office place. First, let's look at what might cause the tension, some basic differences between Boomers and GenXers. In communication, bosses Jennifer and Christopher probably grew up with e-mails and text messages; Boomers prefer face-to-face meetings and the telephone. Instead of looking at e-mails (and especially text messages) as rude, recognize their efficiency and ease of contact. Also recognize the difference in work ethic. Boomers stress face time at the office, while GenXers, using the Internet, believe it doesn't matter where the work gets done as long as it gets done. And, if you are like most Boomers, your early bosses were of the drop-down-and-give-me-20 drill sergeant types. GenXers are more laid back. They will give you basic directions and then leave you alone. Adapt to this longer leash; you just might like it.

Now realize that I didn't tell you to just roll up and die. There does needs to be some assertiveness on your part to inform you boss of your value. Although your boss is younger, you have plenty to offer—experience, maturity, and the knowledge of how things will often pan out. In addition, your experience has created a talent of multitasking, the ability to juggle several projects and priorities simultaneously. You probably have a well-developed and extensive network of personal and professional contacts. Focusing on these strengths, traits, and abilities may ease any feelings of insecurity towards your boss. Do not be shy to let him know that you possess good skills and talents. Let him or her know what successes you have had in your career.

You should be proud of what you have done in the past—these things demonstrate the quality of employee you really are. But you just can't rest on this with a younger boss. He is, of course, most interested in what you are going to do for him. So it is especially important that you bring all skills and knowledge current. Know and speak the current jargon and use anecdotes that speak to the present. (Avoid references to Jimmy Carter, Archie Bunker, Woodstock, and Andy Warhol.) It is critical that you have current technological skills; attend courses that will bring you into the modern world quickly. And then, to make it obvious that your skills are up-to-date, ask your boss if you can teach a course to any workers who need their skills updated.

And, one last thing. You are not the only one who may feel insecure in this relationship; there is a good chance your boss may seem insecure too. Think about being in his shoes for a moment. He is possibly in his first management assignment or at least very early in his management career. And now here he is, faced with a worker who is twice his age with four times the experience. He knows you are watching him even closer than his boss is. It's easy to see how he could perceive you as a threat.

You must go out of your way to take this threat away from him. Not by acting incompetent, for sure, but to make it clear that you respect him, his talents, and his authority. Make it clear that you know you have learned things from him. Be clear that you are not interested in a new position (if that's the truth.) Let him know that you will be glad to advise him and share your experience with him behind closed doors. Compliment him behind his back; say positive things about him to his boss. Go out of your way to sincerely make the point that you are not a threat to his career. This, in itself, should do the trick and invite a healthy relationship between you and your younger boss.

Here is a bit of trivia I find quite insightful. The authors of some of the most popular children's books never had children of their own! Margaret Rey, J. M. Barrie, Margaret Wise, Lewis Carroll, C. S. Lewis, and Dr. Seuss (as well as child-raising guru Dr. Benjamin Spock)—never had kids themselves. Even though they were not parents, they wrote some of the all-time great children's classics. Their lack of experience did not stop these authors from writing books that spoke directly to kids. And just because your boss lacks your years of experience doesn't mean that he still can't be a great boss.

PLAYING GOOD POLITICS

Corporate politics is a lot like cholesterol. There is bad cholesterol and there is good cholesterol. When most people hear the term "corporate politics" they think only of J. R. Ewing. You remember him, don't you? There was more schemin' and backstabbing on *Dallas* than there was drinkin' and sex. I'm going to assume that the people who buy this book would never consider shaping their business career around this type of cholesterol and know you are not disappointed that I'm not going to teach it to you. I'm proud to say that I'm not qualified to do so.

I'm also proud to say that I am an expert on the good uses of politics. How in the world can we put those two words together? Let's understand what politics really is. It is simply the planned interaction between people. If those planned interactions are intended to harm another person so you look good, it's bad politics. But if your plan results in a win-win-win situation (for you, the other person, and your company), then your actions are healthy.

Take a gander at some of these examples of good politics and see how you can incorporate them in your corporate image.

You Look Lovely Today, Mrs. Cleaver

The quickest way to get a supporter is to say good things about them. Before you think I am recommending brown-nosing as a political strategy, just hold on to you heckling. Yes, you want to compliment the person, but not to her face. Compliments are best spoken behind their back.

We'll call this backrubbing; it's the counter strategy to backstabbing. You know how backstabbers are always eventually found out? They say rotten things behind your back and sooner or later their words get attributed to them. It works the same way with backrubbing.

When you notice something notable (and positive) about a coworker or boss, find someone close to the "victim" and tell them your compliment. Track down Amanda's best friend and just casually mention that Amanda's report was just about the finest report you have seen. Now if you say something like that directly to Amanda's face she will just consider it empty flattery. But saying it to a third person who is certain to pass it along assures that your remarks are sincere. Congratulations, Amanda is now a good buddy.

Backrubbing works even better if the "victim" is your boss. Perhaps one afternoon you bump into your boss's boss at the coffeepot. It doesn't hurt to mention that Caroline, your boss, really did a great job motivating all the sales staff at the last meeting. Two things will occur. First your compliment will certainly get back to Caroline and your relationship will solidify. And second, Caroline's boss, who is always looking for candidates for future promotion, now knows that you are a good person to have as a direct report.

While backrubbing a good strategy, it will backfire if your compliments are not sincere. Make certain that you mean every word you say and that you truly are impressed with the subject of your remarks. Otherwise you will come off looking like Eddie Haskel, and that is a sad image to hold.

There's No Need to Fear, Underdog Will Be Here

My wife and I were in a theater watching yet another chick flick. (This happens often because, heck, I like chick flicks. And I am secure enough in my masculinity to admit it.) Two rows up was a group of teenagers who were talking and laughing on their cell phones. They were pretty well ruining the movie for everyone, and my wife encouraged me to shut them up. "Hold on a minute," I said. Sure enough, about a minute later several ladies sitting in front of them turned around and told them to either cut it out or get the hell out. The teens said something snarky and left the theater, leaving us to enjoy our cultural experience.

Here's another political gem for Boomers: Let other people fight unpleasant battles. Now I'm not talking about solving important business problem, indeed you should get in the trenches whenever possible to slay business dragons. No, I'm talking dealing with an inept receptionist or fighting management over a horrible holiday schedule. You can be assured that there are enough people around you who are also unhappy with the situation that one of them will jump into the battle. The problem will be solved, and they will be the one credited for getting a poor single mom fired or for stirring up the whole office or for embarrassing your daughter's friends.

OK Pardner, but You'll Have to Draw First

Think back a few years to when you were six years old. Let's say you and a friend are in your backyard playing with your pet dinosaur when you get into an argument. The name-calling escalates to the point that the other kid screams, "I'm going to tell my mommy!" So the kid runs home and tells his mother that you have hurt his feelings. What does she do? She tells him to quit being a sissy and go back out and apologize or else she'll do something that he'll really be sorry about.

LOSE THE BATTLE, WIN THE WAR

Sometimes you get beat. Or it is obvious that if you fight back you will lose. If that is the case, remember the number one rule of big game hunting: Never wound an elephant. If you find it necessary to shoot, then shoot to kill. If that is not the certain result, then do not even aim the gun. A friend told me the following story:

> At one time in my career I had a ridiculous adversary two levels above me. That's right, my boss's boss. He was having some problems in his department and apparently decided I would make a fine scapegoat. He was gunning for me and one day hit me with a barrage of asinine charges, none of which were true but held no substance even if they were. I was stunned but also remembered that I held a few things in my pocket about him that would seriously derail his career. (Examples of wildly unprofessional behavior, illegal conduct, and even an outright lie he had told the company president.) I approached the head of the HR department with my problem. He actually got excited and wanted to fight. He assured me he could save my job as well as get Bozo in a boatload of trouble.
>
> While it was comforting to know that the HR head was declaring me "in the right," and it was tempting to go into battle with HR at my side, I chose to raise the white flag. I correctly reasoned I could get the guy pulled on the carpet, humiliate him, and possibly open him up to legal problems, but I didn't have enough evidence or clout to actually get him fired. If I had used my big gun, all I would have had is a thoroughly pissed off executive vice president who would be on the constant lookout for finding ways to hang me. A wounded elephant with a long memory. That would not have been a victory.
>
> So, I decided to get out of the poisonous atmosphere. Instead of fighting I used my scandalous information to secure a rather cozy severance agreement. Eventfully I went to work at a great job for someone I respected deeply. I lost the battle but won the war.

Other than the mass extinction of dinosaurs, little has changed over the last 50 years. Because bosses, and especially the HR department, hate dealing with interpersonal conflict, the first person to complain usually loses. Remember this if you have somebody riding your backside, especially if it is a younger worker trying to "get under the old man's skin." If your errors are minor or even nonexistent, encourage the little sissy to go tell his mommy. Say, "Wow, Christopher, I can tell this is really bugging you. You know what I would do if I were you? I'd go tell HR how I felt." You win either way with this method. Bullies are cowards, and the little weasel will probably just back off, knowing that you just called his hand. Or, in the unlikely event that he takes you up on his offer, HR will undoubtedly chastise him and enter some unflattering notes into his personnel folder. And you will come out of the whole episode looking confident, reasonable, and mature.

Jed, Somebody Needs to Shoot That Li'l Whippersnapper

There are some people who are alive only because it's against the law to kill them. You'll run across a few of these varmints from time to time, especially if you are trying to just mind your own business, do your job, and not make waves. How do you handle the (usually) younger worker who is trying to build himself up by tearing you down? Probably the best method is not to kill him; instead turn him into an ally.

Here's what you do. The next time you head a project, ask for Jennifer to be placed on the work team. Pull her aside and tell her that you believe she is the most underrated executive in the company. Lay it on thick, point out some of her true skills. Tell her how you need her advice and help to make the project a success. (Again, make sure these comments are true and sincere.) The fact is everyone likes to be recognized for their talents, and they especially like the people who do the recognizing. In addition, shared struggles and shared victories tend to bond soldiers, baseball players, and coworkers.

And then, shovel it on real thick. When you present this successful project to management, again shower Jennifer with praise. Point out her specific contributions. Have her grinning like a Cheshire cat. Are you worried about making her look too good? Nah. Management knows who was in charge, and they also know what a pain she is. They will give you full credit not only for the successful project but also for taming the wild beast.

As Reported by Walter Cronkite

Some of you will remember a U.S. Senator named Everett Dirksen. Senator Dirksen was the minority leader during the administration of Lyndon

Johnson. Even though Republicans were a tiny minority in those days, Dirksen was able to win many important battles by using this method.

It seems that whenever the Senate would hold a vote on a bill and his personal vote would not make any difference in the outcome, Dirksen would vote with the losing side. Why vote with the losers? He explained: *The victors never remember and the defeated never forget.* Later, when he was trying to scrape up some votes for an important piece of legislation, he would pay a visit to some fellow Senators and remind them of his support during their defeat. They were usually eager to repay his kindness.

I have remembered this my whole career. I flock to people who have been chewed out, chewed up, fired, or defeated. I make it a point to be there whenever someone is at a low point. Remember this, those who are down will be back again. And when they climb back, they will remember you. You will be known as the kind, compassionate, and mature person in the company. What a great reputation for a Boomer!

Chapter 6

Wrong Job, Right Company: Strategies

Here's a scenario that is not unusual. You love the company you work for. Perhaps you have been there for years and the location is an easy drive from your home. The company is solid financially, management is creative and honest, and it produces products or services that you believe in. Yes, things could not be better at work. All is well except for one detail—you absolutely hate the job you do.

Perhaps you have been doing the same thing over and over and are now in a rut. Or maybe you have been at the same level for too long and need a greater challenge. Whatever the cause, stagnation has set in and that, mixed with the onset of middle age, is a deadly combination.

First, let me congratulate you on diagnosing the problem as with your job and not your company. Too many people find themselves in this rut and immediately strike out at the whole organization instead of looking a little closer to home. It's interesting that there is remarkable similarity here between jobs and marriage. The divorce rate is so high because they blame the entire relationship instead of a small irritant that could be changed. But again I digress.

It's smart to find a way to change your job instead of losing the whole company. You have a lot of equity there. You've probably built up some seniority and have moved into the next tier of vacation time. You know the system and how things work both officially as well as the unwritten rules. Relationships are solid, you understand the people and know how they'll react to various situations. You've built important customer contacts. Most important, all these people also know you. If you were to change companies you would have to rebuild all the relationships and your reputation. That's spending a lot of time getting reestablished that you could better use for other things.

There are a few ways to scratch the itch you have. You can get promoted, make a change laterally, or simply enrich the job you have. Let's look at some possible ways to deal with job unhappiness other than throwing away your whole company.

ENRICH

There is an uncomplicated way to deal with an unfulfilling job and that is to make it more fulfilling. I don't want to state the obvious or play word games, but often the job might be great if there was just one little improvement to the job description. Evaluate what is missing and add it to your duties.

Often these changes can be made without even getting permission or by simply letting the people affected know your plans. For instance, appoint yourself the head of the new company softball team and organize the program. Or decide that the stockroom is a mess and ask the branch manager if you can organize it and handle all purchasing. There is a broad range of scenarios here, but the point is that you can probably make a lot of simple changes in your position without a whole lot of hoop-jumping.

Minor tweaks might not be what you had in mind. You may need a bit more octane than that scenario. Not a problem; your boss will be delighted to hear it. Walk into you boss's office, tell her what's on your mind, and ask for significant new responsibility. Together, the two of you should lay out your talents and interests and construct a plan to add real challenges to your job. One way to do this is to approach her as a new product or new client or new process is coming to your company. Ask to be given significant responsibilities there.

Or simply look over elements of her job that she would love to get rid of and volunteer to pick that up for her. "I was based in the same office as my regional manager," Richard explained. "I noticed that she grumbled each month as the deadline for the monthly report to corporate approached. My boss had a lot of talents and skills, but writing and the process needed to produce a good status report sure wasn't one of them. So it was an easy sell to get her to let me take over that duty. Besides the fact that I scored some real points with the boss, I admit that I rather enjoyed the new duty. I got to interact with my peers, had access to a lot of interesting information, as well as learned much more about the company."

MOVE OVER

Sometimes you need more of a change than just additional duties. Sometimes you need to simply replace those duties with a whole new job description. Time to switch fields altogether.

Janet was an employee of a local police department where she headed the public desk at a local precinct. As a civilian employee, sometimes she felt like she had all of the hassle of being a police officer without any of the clout. "People would come in and want to file a complaint against a neighbor because every night he played his stereo too loud," she explained. "I'd tell him that he couldn't just file a report like that in the middle of the day when nothing was happening. He needed to wait until tonight and have an officer come witness it." Janet continued, "That would make the person mad and usually result in him accusing me of calling him a liar or not caring about the public. I just got tired of the abuse. At least if I were a cop I would have the pleasure of writing them a ticket."

So how did Janet handle the frustration? "I got out of there," she said. "I stayed with the police department but transferred over to finance with a great accounting job. I still work in the same building, get to see all my friends, and have held on to my seniority, but now my blood pressure has dropped at least 20 points."

Consider doing what Janet did. Don't move out, move over. Are there other departments in your company that seem to draw your interest? Nothing says you need to sit behind the same desk doing the same darn thing your whole career. Do what it takes to move to the other desk. Here are some steps to make that happen.

Enlist Help. Don't keep your desires secret. Immediately tell your boss what is on your mind and ask for her help. If she is a credible executive, she'll understand and offer to help. She'll give you candid feedback on what you need to do and contact the other department to solicit their support. Also, get HR fully involved. They can help you put together a plan and help you acquire the skills you need.

Acquire the Skills You Need. If you are like Janet and already have the necessary accounting degree, a transfer will be much easier to arrange, but if the barrier preventing a transfer is as significant as a missing degree, jump right in and get it done. Don't let major obstacles scare you off. There is a classic "Dear Abby" column in which a lady explains why she's not bothering to go back to school, "At this pace it'll take me seven years to finish my degree and I'll be 55 years old by then." Dear Abby replied: "How old will you be in seven years if you don't get your degree?"

So do what you need to make the change you desire. But don't just jump the major hurdles, take care of all of them. Perhaps you just need a few courses or need to learn a new computer program or have 500 hours of flight experience, or whatever. When working with your boss and HR on your plan, put all the needed credentials on a calendar and work your plan. Another benefit of doing this is instant gratification. You might find that the process of working toward the new job is as satisfying as the new job itself.

MOVE UP

President Calvin Coolidge was a man of few words. For instance, at the end of his first full term he called a press conference and handed each newsman a card that simply read, "I do not choose to run." A newspaper writer boldly asked him the obvious follow-up question: Why not? "Because there is no opportunity for advancement," the president replied.

The natural transition of every career is to move up. Boomer desires are no different. When we consider moving up, we think of two ways to do that: finding a "better" job and getting promoted in your present company. Moving out is discussed in detail in chapter 7; we'll discuss moving up right here. Let's look at some good strategies for building your career in your present company, in other words, getting promoted.

You can walk into your office with your eyes closed. It's noon before you have to wake up. Your life is on cruise control and you aren't seeing the substance in your job you once did. You love your company but you are unchallenged and often bored. Time to move up.

Master Your Current Job

This hint is actually not as obvious as it may seem. In theory, promotions do not occur because you are doing a great job where you are, they occur because your superiors believe you will do a great job in another, higher position. Realize that in most organizations these days, a boss is not a super employee. The boss is not expected to be able to produce more widgets that a line employee, draft better ad campaigns than his agency employees, or get more hits than his centerfielder. No, if that were the case, instead of being a boss he would just stay in that position and be paid a lot more.

No, a boss is not a super employee. His is a different job. It is a job with a broader scope looking out after a bigger picture. Yes, the boss needs a firm understanding of the subordinates' jobs, but certainly doesn't need to be the most skilled. As an executive with Long John Silver's you can be assured that I knew how to perform every line position, but you can also bet the farm that I was nowhere near the fastest hushpuppy cooker in the company. Alex Rodriguez may be the best third baseman in the game, but no one is considering making him the third base coach.

So, if a boss doesn't need to be the best employee in the organization, why am I telling you to master your job before you can get promoted? Because it doesn't look good to promote someone to greater responsibility when he is unable to handle the responsibility he has now.

Make certain your own personal house is in order before looking to move up. Understand that by saying that you should master your job I am not telling you to be the best. (Remember Alex Rodriguez.) What I am saying is that you should be competent in all areas, have no significant weak spots. Be cloaked in that image of competency in your present situation before declaring your candidacy for more responsibilities.

Have the Full Set of Skills

Few people get promoted by accident. The promotions usually occur when you have acquired the skills necessary in the new job and it appears you are a better fit than any of the other candidates that are being considered.

Remember, the next job is not just an accelerated version of the job you have now; it has its own scope. Let's say you are a marketing specialist responsible for designing newspaper advertisements. The next job up for you is director of marketing. This bigger job certainly requires the understanding of advertising design (which is why you need to be fully competent) but also envelops many more aspects. The director must know how to budget, negotiate, and deal with other media in addition to newspapers. The director must also be able to manage, guide, and motivate a staff. Acquiring these skills is necessary to manage the whole department.

How do you get those skills and demonstrate your competence? One way is to go out and get any training or education you may be lacking. In-house programs and local colleges are great places to get what you need. Another way is to just ask coworkers about what they do and have them show you some of the easier to master ideas. But the best way can be by just being exposed to the activity. Most projects require multidisciplinary teams to get accomplished; work side by side with your peers and see how the work fits together. Often this is adequate to have a good working knowledge of the bigger picture.

Over Instead of Up

Consider a transfer if a job higher up is not available or, especially, you are not ready for the job. Sometimes the list of skills you need to acquire might look overwhelming and merely being exposed to them is just not enough. Ask your boss or the HR department to move you into a new position in the same department that will help round out your package. This is also a good move if the position you have an eye on is filled by someone who looks like he isn't going anywhere for a while. Move to some new scenery, get a new routine, and conquer a new set of challenges. In any event, a lateral move can give you some new experiences to round out your resume.

Make a Plan

One of my favorite sayings is the old Yiddish proverb, "Man plans, God laughs." Here is an example where a man made a plan that involved us all laughing, as well as the planner laughing all the way to the bank.

Remember the dogfight to replace Johnny Carson back in 1991? Hosting the *Tonight Show* was the most desirable job in the entertainment business. Lots of people wanted the spot but it became apparent that it would come down to two: David Letterman, host of the show that followed Carson; and Jay Leno, the "permanent guest host" of the *Tonight Show*. All the smart money was on Letterman. He was a favorite of the NBC executives and wildly popular with his viewers, and it was pretty well understood that Johnny Carson was his mentor. Despite this obvious choice, Leno got the job.

How did that happen? While Letterman waited for Carson to place the crown on his head, Leno worked a plan. Leno realized the clout that local NBC affiliates had over the network. To curry their favor, he used his heavy travel schedule to include appearances on their local morning shows whenever he was in their town. After making hundreds of such appearances, Leno was by far the affiliate owners' most popular NBC entertainer. When the time came to decide, those affiliates were able to overrule any decision made by the programming director, NBC executives, or Johnny Carson himself. Jay Leno grabbed the top spot in television by making a great plan and working it hard.

Make a plan for being promoted. First study the job you target and all of its elements. What are the required qualifications? Pick up any you are lacking, such as education, special training, or unique skills. As we mentioned earlier, become familiar with the jobs of all the positions that report to this one. Interact with the people the target position would have you interacting with. You get the idea.

Also make a visit to the HR department and enlist its help. HR can fill you in on the skills you need to learn and things you need to know. They can help arrange workshops and special assignments. Simply put, HR can not only help you build your plan, they can also put you in the situations you need to fulfill the plan.

Follow the System

There are some organizations where you don't have to put together a plan; they already have one and you just need to follow their system. An extreme example can be found with many unionized companies. Promotions in blue-collar jobs are heavily dependent on seniority. This is often true for positions not covered by the union contract. (I guess the habit gets entrenched; besides it sure is easier to make promotion decisions when all you have to do is look at a calendar.)

A similar situation exists in companies with a heavy internal culture. For a long time the saying was that Sears hired a new stock boy whenever the chairman of the board retired. Some companies are so dependent on internal promotion that they often resemble the rules of succession for the British monarchy. Think carefully before joining such a culture. You may not enjoy a system that considers talent and competence to be much further down the list than time served.

Government organizations, especially at the federal level, have well-established routes to the top. Their qualifications and pathways are carefully spelled out and often dogmatically enforced. If you are part of the post office system, the military, a police department, or any government agency, study their promotion rules and procedures carefully. The system is the system, and in these organizations you will be looked upon with suspicion if you try to make your own path. Government organizations don't celebrate trailblazers.

You don't have to be in the government or a union environment to have a promotional system in place. Every company with a solid HR department will usually have some sort of program or system for moving up. Some programs may be formal and even include internal workshops and company-sponsored courses. Others might be informal, that is, they have an unspoken system that is customary to follow. These types of cultures will often speak of "having your ticket punched." By that it means that you should go through certain experiences before expecting to move up in the organization. If this is the case, meet with your boss and the HR department and memorialize the pathway on paper. If the company has a route in place, follow it.

Market Yourself

Some people feel uncomfortable with the concept of marketing themselves, feeling a bit like Herb Tarlek at WKRP. Of course, good marketing and good selling are rarely about the "hard sell"; you certainly don't want to draw attention to yourself in that manner. Think of a much softer—almost routine—approach that slowly builds a great impression. Here's what I mean.

Instead of constantly pounding your boss with *look-what-I-dids*, subtly keep her informed of your progress on various projects and priorities. And I do mean subtle. Each encounter should add new information, and when you can, fold the message into the day's news. For example: "I just spoke with a solid candidate for the accounting job. We're making contact with some really impressive people." Painless, isn't it? While not much in itself, a regular diet of these interchanges will give you an image of competence as well as for being a positive person who is focused on the company's needs.

Also, you may think you of your relationship with your boss as being one-on-one in nature, but it's actually more complex that that. You are one part of a small society surrounding her. This society includes your peers, your boss's peers, your boss's boss, customers, suppliers, and so forth. They all influence your boss's impression of you. Their comments, attitudes, and impression of you will inevitably affect your boss's opinion of you and your work. Make sure that you work just as hard to develop a positive impression with all members of this society. You want to ensure that when it comes time to move up, the entire organization has a good impression of you.

Be Visible

Make it easy for management to see you in the bigger role and as part of the group that tends to hold higher positions. One way to do that is to be seen frequently around the people who will be your peers when you do get promoted. Offer to sit in for your boss whenever she is unable to attend a meeting of her peer group. Volunteer to represent your department on any cross-discipline committee or work group. Make presentations before senior management, author reports and analyses, attend any workshops that you know your boss or her peers will be attending. Raise your hand when management asks for a volunteer to head the safety committee, or head up the office Christmas party. The point is for you to be visible to the people you will be associating with after you get that promotion.

The Simplest Way to Get a Promotion

Here is an interesting fact about me: I hold the lowest elected political office in the state of Georgia. The fact is even the proverbial dogcatcher outranks me. Despite that humble ranking, I can still take pride in the fact that I was elected (and re-elected by an impressive landslide, I might add) to a political office. That is something not too many people can say. But you know why most people can't say it? It's because most folks have never stuck their neck out and asked anyone to vote for them. Most people don't hold a political office simply because they never asked for the job!

It works that way in the office, also. You might be surprised at the number of people who believe that they will get a promotion just by doing a great job and keeping their noses clean. They figure that when an opportunity comes around, upper management will remember how qualified they are and be convinced that they will be the right fit for the position. Now intellectually, we all know that is simply not a workable plan; however, in actual practice, it is the way too many people approach the task of getting promotion. They will sit by benignly, watch the fellow in the next cubical pass them by, and eventually work up the courage to complain. And they are shocked, *shocked!* when they are told, "Promotion? I never knew you were even interested!"

You can't be promoted if no one knows you want to be. The simplest way to get promoted—and really the only way—is to ask for the job.

CONSIDER A CAREER COACH

During the 1990s, the "in" thing was to have a therapist. This was in keeping with the trend of being a victim, I suppose, but at cocktail parties you could hear the snobby refrain, "My therapist said . . ." or "I discovered in therapy yesterday that . . ."

People don't seem to be name-dropping therapists much anymore, but there does seem to be a new, positive trend. It would seem that nowadays everyone has a career coach.

Career coaching is the hottest new field in consulting. A Google search for this term will return tens of thousands of responses. These coaches come from diverse backgrounds and offer products that vary just as much. The term "career coaching" seems to cover the spectrum from psychiatric counseling to resume writing. A career coach can serve as anything from a mentor to a personal public relations agent to all points in between.

Career coaching is a relatively new profession. There are no government standards or regulations concerning its practice and no barriers preventing anyone to claiming that title. Ergo there are a lot of charlatans thrown in with the solid professionals and a lot of mediocrity mixed in between. You have to sort them out to ensure you are getting the help you need from someone who knows what she is doing. Here are five questions to ask a potential coach that will help you do just that.

How Do You Define "Career Coach"?

People cloaking themselves with term may come from many different perspectives. Some consider themselves psychologists while others might take the role of a job placement firm. Some try primarily to help you find your direction in life, while others see themselves as your own personal board of directors as you climb the corporate ladder. Still others see their role as meeting you where you are and providing the tools and advice you need at this stage of your career. Make certain the coach's perspective matches what you need.

How Will You Develop My Program?

Hacks will have a one-size-fits-all approach. They will pull a program off the shelf and try to fit you within their mold. You don't want that of course, but neither do you want to retain someone who claims to be able to deal with every possible situation. You don't want a motivational goal setter to guide you when you need help positioning you within your existing corporation. Make certain your coach will mold the program to you and address your specific needs.

How Do You Measure Your Success?

This question will confirm whether your coach is focused and has a good understanding of your situation and needs. If she had a hard time defining career counselor, she'll have an even tougher time explaining this one. A professional will be focused and know exactly how to define her success in working with you.

What Is Your Fee Structure?

Large fees up front are a dead giveaway for a scam. Do not let someone seduce you with the health club pitch: Yes, *it is a big commitment. But this way you will not drop out and you will stick with the program since you have paid so much for it!* A small up-front registration fee is reasonable (there are a lot of costs associated with bringing on a new client) as is a cost for initial testing. But ongoing services should be paid by the session. You should be able to stop at anytime and not have to sign an ongoing contract.

What Are Your Credentials?

The government does not license career coaches or counselors so you will have to develop your own set of credential requirements. Examine her resume; evaluate education and experience. Ask for references, and follow up with a few phone calls. While it is entirely possible to be a legitimate and effective career coach without belonging to a professional association, membership in the National Career Development Association or the National Board of Certified Counselors should be considered a big plus.

And Two to Ask Yourself

You will be spending a great deal of time with this coach. You'll be exploring your desires and goals and issues and hopes and dreams. So ask yourself: Do I trust her? Do I like her? For your relationship to work you must enjoy working with the coach and feel comfortable sharing your thoughts and feelings. If there is a wall there between the two of you, the relationship is just not going to work. On the other hand if communication flows easily and there seems to be a good mutual respect, congratulations! This has the framework of a productive relationship for you.

Career coaches are not for everybody. Hire one if it fits, but never just because you want to fit in with the vogue cocktail party chatter.

Chapter 7

Right Job, Wrong Company: Strategies

Here is a point most Boomers will reach at least once in your career: You love your job but cannot stay with your company. There may be several reasons for needing to leave your present company. They may initiate it by laying you off or even firing you. Or it might be your decision—you can't stand your boss, or the company might make a decision that you cannot live with, or you simply need more money. Or, as is becoming more normal in today's society, your spouse has been transferred and you are moving from Heaven, Hawaii, to Hell, Michigan. No matter what the stimulus, your situation is not unique. You need to find a similar position at a new company.

There is a lot of overlap between advice for finding a new job and changing careers. Much of the search information is similar, such as networking, interviewing, building your resume, and sourcing opportunities. Because of this, I've divided those subjects between this chapter and chapter 8, and I recommend that those looking for a new job study both chapters equally.

As we discussed in the first chapter, the world has changed. This is especially true when you are looking for a job. When you first entered the workforce, there is a good chance you found that first job by browsing the newspaper classifieds. Or, perhaps you went to work where your dad worked and just stayed on. Some of you mailed a flurry of resumes to all the big-name employers in town. These methods were somewhat effective 20 or 30 years ago, but you will become quite frustrated focusing a job search on these methods today.

Another source of frustration is listening to some of the common wisdom being bandied about today. For instance, if you follow some advice and "Call around to all the headhunters," you'll become discouraged and actually think you have very little worth on the market. Later in this chapter we'll save you this frustration by explaining how today's headhunters work and how you can use them productively.

More common wisdom leads you to the Internet or to job fairs. Again, these can be used productively, but if you follow the standard approach, you will be sadly disappointed and waste much of your valuable time.

This chapter will explore job search methods that work. More importantly, we'll look at how to use the methods and sources correctly and in an effective fashion. But first, let me hammer home one key point.

THE RATIOS

Here are two ratios you need to memorize.

20:85   80:15

Let me explain:

- Twenty percent of jobs available are advertised. Eighty percent of all available jobs are *never* advertised. Let that soak in a minute.

- Here's another interesting statistic: Eighty-five percent of people looking for jobs only look for them in the traditional advertised job market.

- Do the math. If 85 percent of the job seekers are chasing 20 percent of the jobs, then 15 percent of the job seekers are going after 80 percent of the jobs. (Read that again slowly.) Now, which side of the page do you want to operate in?

- If you have been relying on the Internet and classified ads as your primary sources, this ratio explains why you have probably not been getting much traction.

And that explains why we are going to spend the bulk of this section studying the 80/15 side of things. Of course some people do find a job by looking through newspapers or the Internet, or some other passive method. Then again, sometimes even a blind squirrel will find a nut. So, in honor of those blind squirrels, we'll devote a little bit of time to what I call *passive sources* at the end of this chapter. But right now, let's focus on the *active* sources. And that would be what is often referred to as "the secret job market" or simply, networking.

THE COFFEEPOT: THE MAGIC OF NETWORKING

Actually there is nothing magic about networking except the results. There is nothing complex going on here. You meet with people, tell them about your situation, they give referrals, and you meet some more people. That's about it.

Perhaps that explanation was a bit vague. (It was not unlike Steve Martin's seminar on *How to Own a Million Dollars in Real Estate in Two Easy Steps*. "Step one, get a hold of a million dollars.") Let's go into a bit more detail, but I'm telling you, there's not a whole lot more to it than simply meeting people and talking with them.

Your first step is to make a list. Begin by listing everyone you know in your company and in the industry you have targeted. Add to the list everyone you know who might know someone in your industry. Now there is where the lightbulb goes off. The fact is that just about everyone on the planet possibly knows someone in the industry you are seeking a job in. But to avoid expensive trips to Thailand, lets be a bit more restrictive than that.

Start adding to the list those folks who tend to get to know a lot of people during the course of their day. List the lady who sold you your home. Your pharmacist, insurance agent, and pastor would be excellent additions. And then there's . . . old friends.

Here are some more categories to help jog your memory. Set up a booklet or a Word document, and list these categories at the top of each page. Then as you think of people fitting the category, write them down. An even better idea—use index cards. Carry the cards with you as you go about your daily business and jot down the names as they occur to you.

• friends	• community associations
• neighbors	• banker
• relatives	• accountant
• coworkers	• alumni group
• customers	• church/synagogue/mosque members
• suppliers	• lawyer
• your stack of business cards	• doctor
• your state representative	• spouse's connections

SPECIAL FOCUS: OLD FRIENDS

Building a good network begins by approaching your friends. You need to ask for their help. Contact casual acquaintances, even people you haven't spoken with since your college days. Does that make you uncomfortable? Let's turn the tables. Suppose you are at home one night and the phone rings. It's an old college bud who you haven't talked with in 20 years. He tells you he is in a job transition and would appreciate your advice. Question: would you take a few minutes and try to help him? Of course you would. So why not give that friend the same show of respect. Give him a chance to be there for you.

Now that you have made one heckuva long list, it is time to pick up the phone and make some calls. Your approach is simple, conversational, and *truthful*.

> *As you may have heard, I am in a career transition and I need some advice. I'd appreciate meeting you for coffee later this week, telling you a bit about me and my search, and getting your advice on a few questions I have for you.*

You should have no problem getting these appointments. Here is the reason for this. People love to be asked for advice. It is flattery at its highest. You are showing deep respect for someone when you ask for their opinion and insight, and just about anyone will enjoy being placed in that position. But you may be met with some resistance from time to time. Sometimes a contact might misunderstand your purpose and think you are asking them for a job. Reassure the contact by saying something on the order of:

> *I have no reason to think that you even know about any possible jobs. That's not why I want to meet. I'd like to meet, swap ideas, and get your advice.*

Note that you are speaking the truth. You don't expect the initial contacts to have a job, or even know of a job. The system rarely works that way. How it eventually does work is in the second or third generation of contacts. You'll often get a call out of the blue from someone you have never even met; someone you did meet with a few weeks earlier passed your name along. But I am getting ahead of myself. Let's look at other potential contacts available to you.

When you tell them you are only looking for advice—and not asking for a job—most anyone will take the time to meet you and become acquainted. This is also how you can meet the big names in industry. Highly successful people often became highly successful people because of who they know. While the success rate for meeting those you are already acquainted with (or referred to) is about 95 percent, perhaps the success rate for meeting company presidents you don't know will be about 60 percent. That's a darn good rate for meeting with people who have networks running into the thousands.

Don't believe me? I have found that the higher a person's rank, the easier it is to get in contact with them. Possibly that is because successful people have learned it is best to be easily accessible. Now is not the time to be shy. *Remember: you are not inconveniencing someone when you ask for advice. In fact, you are paying her a huge compliment.*

Now let's talk about the meeting itself. Ideally, arrange to meet for coffee. The office is fine, so is lunch, but coffee usually presents the best overall venue. The atmosphere is relaxed, yet professional and you don't have to worry about a lot of interruptions. (Remember to silence your cell.) So, how do you conduct the meeting? First remember the basics:

- This is not a job interview.
- Have no expectation that the person you are speaking with even knows of any job openings.
- There is no grade. You will not pass or fail this meeting. Relax, it's a business meeting. Really.

What are your objectives?

- You want to meet people in your industry and build a business relationship with them.
- You want some questions answered. You want some advice.
- You want some referrals of others you can talk with.

Here are some more important points in holding these discussions.

- Keep it under an hour. If more needs to be discussed, set up another meeting another time. *Note:* This is one of the areas most advisors disagree with. They will suggest the meetings be held to 20 or 30 minutes. I disagree with those severe restrictions because not much can be done in 20 minutes. Pleasantries have just barely been exchanged and not much bonding has taken place before it's time to wrap up the discussion.

Let me tell you how all this effort will eventually end. One afternoon you will be in your office, probably grumbling to yourself about hitting a dead end or such, and the phone will ring. On the other end is a person you have never spoke to or even heard of. She will mention that she is with a company and that she heard that you might be a good fit for a position that just came open and would like to talk with you. Now where do you think she got your name? Probably around the coffeepot.

This is where this method is often called the "secret job market." When a spot comes open in a company, management's first reaction is to fill it with referrals rather than placing expensive ads or paying headhunter fees. A typical scenario would be this: Jan, the director of marketing, just had her top advertising executive quit suddenly. She walks down the hall and pours a cup of coffee. She bumps in to Phil, the purchasing manager, and mentions the recent loss. "Hey, you don't happen to know anyone who could do that job, do you?" she asks. Phil takes a sip of his coffee, thinks for a moment, and then replies, "You know, I might. A couple of weeks ago I met this fellow who seemed pretty sharp. He had a lot of advertising experience with some top companies. You might want to give him a call."

Now three things are going on here. First, Jan sees a chance to fill the position quickly without a lot of hassle or expense. Second, you have an opportunity to interview for a job you wouldn't have otherwise known about (and with no other competition). And Phil? He gets to be a hero, not just in your eyes but also to a coworker high up in the organization. Win-win-win.

Far fetched? Nope. That's how 80 percent of the jobs are filled.

YOU ARE IN LUCK IF YOU HAVE BEEN LAID OFF

Sometimes harmful events allow special privileges. And for those of you who have been laid off from your previous job, I have good news for you. A whole new universe of great referrals is now available to you. These are referrals that would not be available if you were still employed with your previous company.

Here are some examples:

- *Executives and employees of your previous company.* If you were still working for the company that laid you off, you would not be able to tap into the referrals and advice all their employees have to offer. But now that you are not, make liberal use of your previous work family. Add them all to your network; in fact make your ex boss the first person you visit with over a cup of coffee. Chances are good he and all the other management you know can offer some great referrals.

- *Board members.* The members of your company's board of directors had to approve your layoff. Trust me, they feel guilty about this. Play on that guilt. These men and women hold positions of great power in their own companies and will want to help you find a new position, possibly with their company. Regardless, anyone who has attained a board membership has developed an impressive network. Ask them to share it with you.

- *Suppliers.* Yours is not the only company your vendors and suppliers work with. They have been inside the operations of similar companies and have built a relationship with them as close as the one they have with you. (Which is yet another reason to treat your purveyors with courtesy and respect.)

- *Franchisees.* Did you work for a company that has franchisees? Jackpot. Your franchisees are really just a small version of the parent company. Meet with the franchisees. Remember, you don't have to personally know them. It'll be easy to find a way to network to them.

- *Competitors.* Competitors would be delighted to talk with you, if for no other reason than they think they can learn a lot about your company from you. (Ethics on this: It's fine to talk about issues in general, but never bleed any confidential or proprietary information.)

THE INSIDE REFERRAL

Let's look at another powerful number, 42. You are 42 times more likely to get a position if an existing employee refers you than to get a position you applied for without an internal referral. Let that soak in a minute. It is an amazing number. Here's a question for you. When applying for a job, why wouldn't you use a referral to get inside the company? Perhaps you may say, "Because I don't know anyone who works there." To which I would reply, "Re-read the previous section."

Here is your goal. You want to be referred to one of your target companies by someone that knows you and also knows someone inside your target company. Why is that? Because executives pay a lot of attention to people referred to them by someone they know. Such a referral serves as a recommendation; the executive assumes that "if Katherine recommended her, she must be as good a worker as Katherine." (Of course, this may backfire if Katherine is an obnoxious slacker.)

In a moment, we'll use the basic Coffeepot system to get inside target companies. But first we need to identify the companies you want to target. How do we make this selection? The first thing you need to do is determine the criteria for a company to make your list. You won't want to use all of these, just those that are important to you in deciding where you want to spend the next several years of your life. Consider:

- type of industry
- size of company
- location
- environment
- reputation
- profit/nonprofit status
- any other criteria that are important to you.

Now get ahold of a business guide in the area you are searching. Most major cities have such a guide that lists all the businesses in the area broken down by many of the criteria just listed. Also make liberal use of Internet search engines to find such lists.

Then make a list of companies to contact. List between 200 and 400 potential employers. Yep. I said 200 to 400. Why so many? One reason is that it is your goal to find every company that may possibly offer you a job that meets your qualifications. Secondly, while conducting such an extensive search you will discover many more possible employers that don't make the big lists. This is true for many new or small companies (which few of your competitors are contacting).

DOUBLE BONUS

Keep your eyes open to learn of those companies that offer their employees a referral bonus. If a company does pay cash to employees who find new employees, then every employee of that company becomes a superb contact for you. Not only will they pass along your name, they will be doing everything they can to get you hired.

Rank the companies according to your criteria, with the number one company listed first on your target list. Add new companies to the list as you hear of them. This is similar to networking contacts insofar as how the list expands. As you research a company, you'll find out about its competitors and suppliers. You will be amazed at how quickly the list expands with great companies.

Now, it's time to use the Coffeepot system, slightly modified for special targeting. Identify people you know that work for any of the targeted companies or contact people you know that know people at the targeted companies.

Invite these new friends to coffee. Simply tell them that you are in a job transition, have reason to believe that their company would be a good place to work, and say you have a few questions about the company and its culture. Ask out about people at the company, current hot buttons and the names of department heads that you ought to be talking with. Finally, ask permission to use their name when you inquire.

A lot of work? Not really. Especially when you realize that one contact using the name of a referral equals 42 cold, faceless contacts.

PASSIVE SOURCES

Despite the fact that the jobs are fewer and the road much more crowded, many people do indeed find their next career step in the newspaper, on the Internet, or by one of the other passive methods we'll discuss here. Yes, it is worth some of your time using these methods, but I urge you—beg you—to invest no more than 20 percent of your time doing so.

Classifieds

During my sophomore year in college, a group of us decided to go to New Orleans for a long weekend. All that stood in my way was getting the $50—a monstrous sum—that I needed for expenses. I called up my dad and asked him to release it from my college fund. He refused, correctly pointing out that the money was only to be used for college expenses. "Get a job," he wisely advised.

So I turned to the only source for finding a job I could think of. I scoured the "Help Wanted—Men" section of the *Memphis Press Scimitar* until I found the perfect situation for an 18-year-old college student with no appreciable skills. I secured a job as a dishwasher at the Pizza Hut. And thus I began a 20-year career in the food service industry, met my future wife, and eventually moved to Atlanta. (No doubt this is an allegory about fate, but it is also a good example of how most people fall into their careers. But once again I digress.)

There was a time when the newspaper classified ads were the primary way of finding a job. In fact, just as in my case, this was probably true for you. But like so many other things, this is just not true any longer. In fact I would venture to say that the newspaper classified has sunk from first to worst on the list of helpful job sources. This change will lead you to severe culture shock if you have not looked for a job in the past 20 years.

That is not to say that the classifieds do not offer any assistance. A wise jobseeker can find some benefit from the classifieds beyond lining the par- rot's cage. For instance many high-level government jobs can be found there since the government often requires their jobs to be posted in "a newspaper of primary circulation." This is also true of many good corpo- rate jobs; EEOC regulations often require the postings for companies with certain government contracts. And, large companies know the newspaper is a great place to troll when they need to hire large numbers of employ- ees, so many entry-level positions can indeed be found there.

With those exceptions, your best use of the local paper is to discover information about job trends. For instance, if a company is opening up a new division in your town, its advertisement for 500 factory workers should tip you off that they'll also be needing many managers, accoun- tants, engineers, and other professionals. (They'll also need many suppli- ers and contractors, if you are considering starting a new business.)

Also, companies rarely advertise all their jobs in one ad. However, if you follow their link back to the company site on the Internet, you will often see a listing of other available positions that they chose to advertise elsewhere.

Trade Journals

Trade journals can be a pretty good source of information about a posi- tion. They will list positions from entry level all the way to upper man- agement, along with a lot of information about the company itself. The drawback? The jobs advertised are usually spread out all across the coun- try. It's tough to find positions in your defined area. Also, since the job is posted for broad distribution, there is a lot of competition. (How do you go about standing out in the crowd? That's right, you network your way inside. Are you seeing a pattern here?)

SHOULD I EVEN BOTHER TO APPLY?

Classified ads are often just a wish list. The person placing the ad thinks he is showing high standards by listing stellar qualifications, but he is actually lowering his standards. Here's what I mean. You are not raising your standards when you require a MBA when actually a BBA is all that's really needed. Instead what you have done is eliminated all the people who hold just a BBA but possess superior skills in the core focus of the job. Often all that's left when you eliminate the BBA candidates is a lone fellow with an MBA, who holds mediocre experience in the very thing you need most.

So when you see an ad you are interested in but the you don't meet all the listed criteria, consider this: if you meet half of the listed qualifications but your experience tells you that you can do the job well, go ahead and apply. There is a good chance you will float to the top of the list. After all, all the other truly qualified people didn't bother to apply.

To expand your search, be sure to study several trade journals across several industries. For instance, if you are a software sales manager, look at journals from all three industries: computers, sales, and management. Another nice feature of trade journals is that many have online directories and online sites. Always check in to these to maximize your exposure to their opportunities.

Some Tricks about Timing Your Inquiry

Here's some great advice for those of you who are like me and miss a lot of deadlines. If you see an ad about four months old, make contact with the company. The heaviest turnover occurs in first 90 days. You just might time it so your inquiry arrives just as the "winner" is packing up his desk.

Also, here is how a lot of searches go for companies that use ads. Many advertisers will have great hopes when placing ads. Accordingly, they think they will raise their standards by requiring traits that make their qualifications sound like the Boy Scout oath. (Trustworthy, loyal, helpful, friendly, courteous, kind; holds MBA, speaks six languages . . .) Because they have such high expectations, they will scrutinize the initial applicants harshly and unreasonably. Then as they have eliminated so many of the early folks, they begin to realize that "perhaps we have overreached." The next applicants they receive start looking pretty darn good. Just like the old Mickey Gilley song says, "The girls all get prettier round closing time." To paraphrase the post office, "Beat the rush. Mail late." How much later? I suggest about a week; however, let's be safe and combine the advice. Go ahead and respond to a desirable ad immediately. Then, wait a week or two and respond one more time.

The Internet

Sounds easy doesn't it? Post a resume, a company finds you, and they call you with a job. Actually, you are more likely to wind up with a mailbox full of people trying to sell you something. The Internet is just not the automatic panacea its reputation would lead you to believe. The competition is ferocious for every job posted. This mess is created because of people who shotgun their resume to every ad posted whether they are qualified or not. (On the hope that if they throw enough against the wall maybe something will accidentally stick.)

Also, so many resumes are posted online that companies must use computer programs searching for key words just to narrow their resume stack to a few thousand. (If your resume doesn't include the magic words, you are toast, no matter how high your quality.) As anyone who has explored the Internet will tell you, searching for a position using this magic tool can be frustrating at best and a big waste of time at worst. Fortunately, the Internet can be of use if you go into it with the tight strategies and realistic expectations.

I recommend that your strategy for the Internet be to peruse rather than post. Here is what I mean. Posting your resume leaves you quite vulnerable to some rotten people with very little hope for success. What kind of hucksters are out there? Prepare to have your mailbox flooded with ads for gambling sites, crackpot medical help, and movie rental plans. Although that is only irritating, you will also receive contacts from people selling lousy advice and assistance for your job search as well as offers of jobs that aren't really jobs. (*For only $1,000 I'll give you an exclusive widget distributorship!*) Even worse are the unprofessional headhunters who shotgun your resume to many companies. (What's wrong with this? I'll explain in the "Recruiters and Agencies" section in a couple of pages.)

However, you will be able to maintain some control if you confine your use of the Internet to looking at the job postings. Use these postings as a starting point. Learn of the opportunity and then do some due diligence before replying. Learn about the company, its products and services, and its reputation before responding. Visit its Web site; you may find more postings there. Another bonus: because of all the knowledge you have gained, your inquiry will stand out from the masses.

Your first instinct may be to head straight for the Big Two job boards (Careerbuilder and Monster), but you may have more success on some of the smaller boards. Look for boards specific to your industry or career path; you won't get lost in weeds so much. Also, I highly recommend that you go to the job board sponsored by your state. (Call your local unemployment office for the Web address.) These are free to use and, better yet, free to advertise on. Why is that such a big deal? Companies pay hundreds—sometimes thousands—of dollars to post a job on the Big Two.

Accordingly, only the bigger companies can afford to post on these sites and then only for a few select jobs. A free service opens things up for the smaller- and medium-sized companies (the source of most jobs in America). Less competition, more jobs—a nice combination.

Another benefit of these sites is that all government jobs must be posted here, as well as many positions offered by companies that hold certain government contracts.

And, a great use of the Internet is to enhance your networking. I recommend LinkedIn as a great site for this. You can post your resume and your profile and link to people you know. You are then automatically linked to people they know and your network quickly builds exponentially. You can use this site to network your way into prospective companies, join groups having similar goals and interests as yours, as well as learn of potential opportunities. Of particular note, many credible headhunters will research and post job openings on this site. Go to http://www.linked in.com/ for a full explanation of their program and some great tutorials on the many ways to use their site.

Job Fairs

Job fairs have been around a long time and their effectiveness varies. Those fairs held by colleges seem to be both effective and efficient. Many companies use these to make both initial contacts as well as follow up on potential entry-level employees. Here's a hint for us Boomers: Go to college job fairs. Not just your alma mater, any you can arrange to attend. Many of the recruiters there have other positions they are also looking to fill and will enjoy the opportunity meet with candidates for positions higher up the food chain.

On the other hand, there are definitely some job fairs to be avoided. Beware of a new scam that seems to be popping up. The scam goes like this: companies rent an impressive facility, invite a few employers, then advertise the heck out of the event. They will make their money by actually charging the attendees, who only discover the scam after they have paid their money and pushed their way into the crowd to find . . . nothing awaits them. Moral: avoid job fairs that make the majority of their revenue from charging attendees. A little job fair will be free or only charge a token fee. The producer should make his money by charging companies that came to interview.

Also, spend your time wisely. Rather than standing in a long line to hand a recruiter your resume, make a list of companies that will be attending. Research these companies ahead of time and (here it comes again) network your way into an introduction. Send your resume to the recruiters before the fair and use the job fair to make your *second* contact. Or if you are not able to get that done before the job fair, use the fair as an opportunity to find out more info, then network your way into an onsite interview later.

I feel silly to even bring this up, but always dress to make a great first impression. For some reason a lot of attendees don't think of these contacts as real job interviews and dress in shorts, T-shirts, and a ball cap. Seriously. Since I'm sure none of the people reading this would do such a thing, I'll chalk this indiscretion up in the "good news" column. Less competition.

Here is my favorite use of job fairs. Practice your networking skills. Learn to overcome any shyness by making it a point to start a conversation with complete strangers. It's a low-pressure way to acquire these social skills as well as often leading to some great referrals. How's that? There is no better way to find out about positions that may be open than to talk to someone who has been out hitting the pavement looking for a job. Think about how many leads you can find chatting to the people attending a job fair. Get these people on your network team!

Free Career Connections

There are a lot of groups out there who want to help you. These range from government agencies, schools, and churches to regional community groups. It is amazing how the length of your job search can be shortened if you take advantage of their services.

Let's start with the aid given by local colleges. As mentioned earlier, you don't necessarily have to be a graduate of a school to take advantage of their services. Many colleges, especially community colleges, receive supplemental grants from the state to operate these centers. Literature, workshops, job postings, and counseling may also be available.

Don't hesitate to visit your state unemployment offices. No, they aren't just for manual labor anymore. States are actively pursuing industry and often partner with new industry as their primary hiring center. Most of the clients at these centers are in our generation and are looking for mid- and upper-level positions. These centers are also a great location for workshops, resume assistance, interview practicing, and (our favorite friend) networking.

Also, check the newspapers for local community groups similar to the Crossroads Career Network. Crossroads is a church-sponsored organization offering a myriad of helpful services. Of note is its Career Explorers' program. This is a seven-week course that rivals the programs of the major outplacement agencies. Counseling and networking opportunities are also offered. Call around to local churches to locate either a Crossroads or similar ministry.

Another great resource: SHRM. Pull out the telephone book (are those things still published?) and locate your local chapter of SHRM, the Society for Human Resource Management. As the name explains, SHRM (pronounced *sherm*) is the professional organization for those in the personnel business. It is an amazingly active association with a great outreach to the community. Call them and ask about their services in your area.

Headhunters, Search Firms, and Agencies

Executive search firms and agencies can be of tremendous value to your career if you are currently employed and not looking for a job; however, if you are unemployed or in desperate need of a job, these same firms may be of little help. To understand this, we must first look at how most search firms operate.

Executive search firms, often called headhunters, are experts at finding great candidates for positions that companies need filling. These firms will be contacted by the hiring company and contracted to acquire candidates for an important position. The firm will use their search methods—usually tapping their network for referrals—to locate two to five candidates for the position. The firm will interview the candidates several times before presenting them to the company, in addition to checking references, testing, and often many other screening services. Once the headhunter is confident that there is a good match, he will present the candidate to the company. The company will then do their due diligence and decide on the person to hire. Then they pay the fee to the headhunter, ranging from 20 to 33 percent of the executive's annual salary.

There are some differences in how firms operate. In some cases the firm will compete with other firms; only the one bringing the successful candidate gets any money. (These are called contingency firms.) And there is quite a variance in the services the firms offer, such as in checking references or negotiating the deal. But no matter which services the firm includes, one feature is constant—the firm always works for the hiring company. They do not work for you.

That is an important thing for you to remember. Though reputable firms will always treat you with respect and are certainly rooting for you, their loyalty is to the hiring company. You are a product, not a client. And it is for these reasons that a search firm can be of great service if you are employed, not so much otherwise.

If You Are Employed, They Are Your Best Buddy

First let's look at the positive side of the equation, that is, if you are currently employed, but interested in looking for a new job. The best way to identify credible executive search companies is to listen for recommendations from your peers. Find out which companies referred them and ask them about their experiences. Then call the company and explain that you are happy and successful in your current position but want to begin a relationship for possible future opportunities. These folks always appreciate directness.

Another way to start a relationship is even easier. Answer your phone. You are probably already receiving a couple of calls a month from headhunters asking for referrals. Spend time with him and do your best to give him the names of people you think he might want to speak with. These referrals don't have to be your best friends. In fact, you may not even know them personally. Just provide the names of people you are familiar with or who have a good reputation in your industry. Providing referrals endears you to any headhunter. He will learn about you and your career desires and will always have you on his mind when something hits his desk you might be interested in.

- Keep the recruiter aware. Send him your updated resume whenever there is a change in status. Drop him a note whenever you have had an accomplishment or if the boss says something notable in your performance review. Send him newspaper clippings of interesting news stories involving your industry. In general, mount a long-term public relations strategy with your headhunter.

- Consider any positions presented to you. Don't wait until you are desperate for a job before looking for one. The fact is fate moves at its own schedule. The ideal job is rarely open when you need it and you must pounce on opportunity when it is presented. I remember numerous executives I had contacted who wouldn't speak to me because "I'm happy where I am now." A few months later the phone would ring and I would hear the familiar story about how they had just been laid off. If they had been open to me a few weeks earlier I could have been a lot of help to them; but by the time they called, I had nothing.

Not as Useful If You Are Unemployed

There are two big reasons that headhunters are not as valuable if you are unemployed. First, as explained earlier, their client company initiates all the firm's assignments. The firm secures an assignment and then begins the search. I worked for several years as a headhunter and found my maximum workload was about four searches. This workload was limited due to the hundreds of phone calls and contacts I would make as well as the many other services I provided to the client company. Now with a caseload of four, what do you think the odds are that I would have a matching situation for you when you called me? Pretty darn slim. In fact,

---

CAUTION! SENSITIVE PEOPLE AHEAD

Since I used to be one (and still occasionally serve in that capacity), I have liberally used the term "headhunter" when describing independent recruiters or executive search consultants. I always liked the term, and even have a collection of pottery heads in my office; however, I've been recently advised that some headhunters are sensitive about the term. They consider it to be derogatory. OK, that's their right, people and groups should be called whatever they want to be called. So to be politically correct, don't use the term in front of a headhunter—I mean *recruiter*—until you hear him or her use it first.

I cannot remember a single match I ever made that was initiated by the candidate contacting me.

The second reason for the lack of helpfulness is how the game is played. Remember, you are a product that the headhunter will be trying to "sell" to the client. It's a shame, but the reality is that your value is severely diminished if you are currently unemployed. The client's reaction is often that unemployed candidates must be "damaged goods" (I know, ouch) or "I could have landed this one on my own, why am I paying you the big bucks?"

Now, after those depressing words, let me dial it back a bit. Search firms are not a complete black hole. Go ahead and contact one or two who specialize in your industry. A reputable headhunter will usually be glad to set aside some time for advice as well as give you a general update on your industry. He may even tell you about some openings at companies that refuse to pay a fee.

And some more good news. You will find a search firm as a golden resource if you are responding to an advertisement placed by a search firm. The fact is, some firms will open things up and try to find candidates through more traditional sources. They'll place an ad on the Internet or in a trade magazine. If you see a position that you are qualified for advertised by a search firm, you have hit the jackpot.

Responding to an outside recruiter is a bit different than dealing directly with an employer. Here are a few tips to help you navigate these new waters.

- Treat the relationship with the firm like a partnership. True, the search firm actually works for the company, but the agency can have some good informal advice for you and your suitability for the job. Besides, you don't want any job that's not a great fit, do you?
- You can discuss difficult issues more openly with a search firm than with a company representative. For instance, it's OK to tell them your salary range or salary desired. They understand that it's best to hold

off on this conversation until the end, but they must know that you are somewhat in the range of the job they've been hired to fill.

- Avoid all the clichéd answers. (Top three? "I'm a people person!" "People say I am firm but fair." "I suppose I work too hard and my quality standards are too high.") They've heard them all.

- Never, ever lie. They will find you out. This is because if you lie to their client the agency's relationship with that company will be destroyed. They cannot risk losing dozens of future searches with a client all because one candidate tried to sneak a credential past them.

✳✳✳

So, now we have a list of some other pretty good sources for finding job opportunities. But let me remind you of the formula we discussed earlier.

20:85   80:15

Remember with these sources, 80 percent of the candidates will be focused on these 20 percent of the jobs. Competition is harsh. Your best bet will be to spend the bulk of your time focused on the networking techniques discussed earlier.

How much time? Since the odds are 80/20 for locating a real job, I suggest you spend no more than 20 percent of your time plowing through the Internet. Why am I so leery of the technology? Because it seems to be so easy to use, I find too many people wasting their whole day in front of a computer instead of working other sources. Networking is hard work, and it's just too easy to get bogged down on the computer. You sit down for a few minutes and when you look up several hours have passed. If you have call reluctance (and don't we all?), the Internet is the greatest excuse ever devised for avoiding picking up the phone. After all, there you are typing away, looking and feeling like you are doing some honest to goodness work, while all you are actually accomplishing is managing to avoid talking to actual human beings on the phone or in person. So order yourself to spend no less than 80 percent of your time networking and no more than 20 percent on these other sources. Actually, I recommend 100 percent of your time networking. Save the 20 percent for late at night. Remember that you can chatter on the computer at midnight, but people get kinda irritated when you call at that time.

Chapter 8

Wrong Job, Wrong Company: Strategies

In the last chapter I told you how I fell into my first career. I needed some cash, applied to the first job I came across, and thus became the dishwasher at a Pizza Hut. Let me tell you the rest of the story. After about six months of pizza making, I became assistant manager at the huge salary of $100 per week. Six months later I became a 19-year-old general manager, setting a Pizza Hut record that can never be broken. (In those days you could sell beer at 18, today you must be 21.) I went on to become a multi-unit supervisor at Burger King; director of operations at a small regional hamburger chain; COO of a chain of hotels, coffee shops, and dinner theatres; then owner of a theatre by the age of 30. After that I spent several years as regional director of about a hundred Taco Bells and then finished the food-service career with Long John Silvers as a regional vice president. I retired from the restaurant industry at 37, ready to scratch a new itch.

I subject you to that biography for a couple of reasons. First, I'm willing to bet that my career journey is a lot like yours. I fell into a career by taking the first job I was offered. Amazingly, that first job was well suited for me at each stage of my career development (which lasted until I was in my late thirties.) This is remarkably how many, if not most, people find their careers. They may be just out of college and take the first position a college recruiter throws their way. Or, like me, they stumble in off the street and miraculously stumble into a career they are actually interested in.

The other reason for the personal story is to point out that these interests—or sweet spots—can change over time. I became bored and stagnant with restaurants when I was 37. I wanted to have my own professional services firm. So I started an HR consulting firm, specializing in executive search. Later my career saw a fork in the road and, as Yogi Berra never said, I took it. I discovered publishers would buy what I wrote, so I began my career as a writer of HR books. About the same time I realized that most employers were wasting their human assets, so my consulting practice switched from finding them new executives to teaching them how to hold on the people they already have. Once again, my sweet spot switched and I switched with it.

There is nothing odd about your urge to change careers. This is especially true at middle age, which is where we Boomers are today. Don't look at this as a middle age crisis. (Unless you are also thinking about divorcing your wife, buying a little red sports car, and driving to Hawaii. In that case, seek professional help.) You made your first career decision when you were about 19 years old. Times have changed and intelligent people change with them. Why? Just think of what your life would be if everything you did was based on a decision you made when you were a teenager.

Let's spend some time discussing that very subject, the importance of finding your sweet spot, and then let's look at how you can find it.

THE SWEET SPOT

An amazing thing happened to me in 1994. I moved to Birmingham. No, that's not the amazing thing; what was magical was what I found on their baseball diamond. This was the year that Michael Jordan left basketball to try his new passion, baseball.

Jordan had signed with the White Sox, and they assigned him to their AA minor league team in Birmingham, the Barons. Let me tell you something about Michael Jordan that probably will not surprise you. Jordan was the consummate professional. He came out early and stayed late to sign autographs and talk with the star-struck kids. On the field he hustled, gave it his very best, and demonstrated an attitude every coach would want on their team. And, he was there for his teammates. He gave what baseball advice he could, and was famous for his support and encouragement for anyone who might be struggling. Michael Jordan was undoubtedly the ideal baseball player, if you were willing to accept his less-than-impressive baseball skills. Sadly, the fact is Michael Jordan just wasn't much of a baseball player.

Think about it a minute. Here is a man who is arguably the greatest basketball player ever. No one has ever dominated a sport the way Jordan dominated basketball. But this incredible athlete, who gave it his all, could not do any better than to be a mediocre minor league baseball player. Finding your sweet spot is just that important to your career.

Actually dramatic misses are not the danger here. You will know a complete mismatch within half an hour of bumping in to one. How long would Bill Gates have lasted as a shoe salesman? Or Donald Trump as a waiter? Or Paris Hilton as a . . . as a . . . as *anything*? No, those mismatches would have become instantly apparent as will yours if you try to shove a square peg into a round hole.

No, the real danger lies in a career that is almost, but not quite, the one meant for you. Michael Jordan playing baseball is a great example. If that had been his first career (and he didn't have a basketball career to compare it to), Jordan might have figured he had found the right career but just wasn't working hard enough. He might have slogged along for a few years, trying harder and harder just to keep his head above water. And what a tragedy that would have been for all of us.

Be very careful not to fall into that rut. If you have to give your job everything you've got just to keep your head above water, time to play a new game. Life—and work—is not supposed to be that hard. Struggle is a prime indicator that you need to move over, perhaps just a few inches, and put your talents and effort elsewhere.

So, how do you know when you've found your sweet spot? My answer is going to disappoint you, so be warned. You find your sweet spot by following your gut instinct. Let me explain this incredible organ we are all blessed with. Your gut is the accumulation of all your instincts, interests, and morals. Your gut has always been with you recording life experiences, making note of what you enjoy and what you despise, activities you love and those you hate. Your gut has accumulated all this personal information and processes it far better than our most advanced computers. You will know you are in the right place because you will be at peace with the decision.

But, you have to give it a little time in order to avoid being seduced by fleeting inspirations. Don't be infatuated with an idea you just met. That's not love, it's a crush. Date the idea for a while, do good research, meet with people in the industry, and let an appropriate amount of cogitation time pass.

Then, follow your gut.

THE REAL CAREER TRAGEDY

The biggest tragedy that can befall your career is not being unsuccessful. The fact is that if you focus on a goal and work hard you will probably succeed. But have you ever known someone who was incredibly successful but still terribly unhappy? Do you know why that is? It's because he picked the wrong goal. The greatest tragedy a Boomer can face *is not* failing to reach the mountaintop. The greatest tragedy is to reach the mountaintop and then discover that you climbed the wrong mountain.

MAKING A CAREER CHANGE

Making a career change is a difficult thing to do. You are turning your back on a field you have worked in for years, possibly decades, and embracing a big unknown. It takes courage to make the leap but if you go about the process in an organized fashion you will greatly shrink the risk. Before committing to your new dream, do some good research, preparation, and strategic planning.

Make Sure You Are Sure. This will take some soul searching. Besides the gut check we discussed earlier, you might want to check out many of the personality tests available, many online. Now don't use these to start from scratch (deciding whether to be a shepherd or professional assassin) but more for additional verification. If the testing and your gut line up, maybe it's time to finally accept the fact that this new direction was meant to be.

Explore the Profession. Perhaps the best way to do this is to modify the Coffeepot method. Take dozens of people out for coffee to explore the profession you have chosen. Ask them questions about their field, their satisfactions, and their frustrations. (Important: *every* career has its frustrations and aggregations. If you never hear anything bad about your chosen field, then you haven't been exploring hard enough. Do a reality check to make sure you are not just in puppy love.)

This round of informational interviews will serve a double purpose. Not only will you get your questions answered, you will also build your network in your new field. That'll become mighty handy when it's time to look for a job.

Get Yourself Some Learnin'. Move ahead with your education. Depending on your field, that might mean anything from graduate school to a few appropriate courses at a technical college to an apprenticeship with a friend. Suppose you begin the training and then change your mind about the new career? Not a problem. The worst that has happened is that you have spent some great time learning a lot about a subject that you are interested in.

Assure Survival. Get a good understanding as to the amount of money you will be making, especially in the early years. Sounds adequate? Check again. We usually overestimate our income and underestimate our expenses at times like this. You don't want to make the giant leap and then realize it just won't cover a minimum lifestyle. (See the book, *Easy Ways to Have Your Spouse Divorce You.*) Here's a way to get a reality check. Try living on the projected income for 90 days.

In the Words of that Famous Philosopher, Nike Adwriter. You have verified your passion, made a transition plan, gotten your skills up to par, and gotten your financial house in order. If the gut still says "Go," then do so. No more procrastination, no more contemplation. Time to make it happen.

CAREER FIELDS WHERE OLDER IS BETTER

What is the right field for you at this stage of your life? Whatever lies at the intersection of passion and abilities. But let's add another criterion to that and look at some career field where age is an asset. Here are four fields where age is identified with wisdom and experience and serves as an asset, not a barrier.

Health Care. Here is a definite trend for the future: demand for health care will only increase as the population ages. This is true not just for doctors and nurses, the positions we think of first when we think of health case, but for the associated services such as administrators, customer service, and technicians. Other health occupations that will likely see an increase in demand include pharmacists and social workers.

While younger people in the medical fields are certainly capable of providing top-quality care and services, some folks just don't like having a doctor half their age making life and death decisions for them. Older health care providers exude a aura of wisdom and good judgment that makes people more comfortable. Most patients, especially the older ones, prefer Marcus Welby to Doogie Howser.

Education. There is a growing demand for math, language, special education, and science teachers, and this demand will only get stronger. This might be a great time to go back to college and obtain your teaching credentials. But, before making this leap, ensure that you have the interest in the profession. With teaching, it's easy to try before you buy: volunteer in your local schools or tutor in your chosen area of expertise.

Parents find a lot of comfort when an older teacher instructs their child. Sure, those right out of college bring a lot of enthusiasm and fresh ideas, but there is much to be said about the passion and life experiences that a Boomer brings to the classroom. I might add that men are now finding the doors swinging wide open for them, especially in elementary schools.

Financial Advisor, Career Counselor, Consultant. If you are looking for a job where people will have faith and trust in your wisdom, look to these advisory jobs where graying hair is a definite advantage. Older people gain instant credibility with stakeholders. Clients natural assume that someone who is older has credibility; this is critical to someone when you are discussing their finances. They figure you are experienced and have been there/done that.

And think about counselors. Would a recent college graduate feel comfortable being mentored by someone who graduated the year before? And the same principal applies to all consultants—age equals experience equals wisdom. (Another good thing about being a consultant—you can consult on just about anything. Once you have reached middle age, you have developed an expertise in many areas. Your background will make clients believe you will commit fewer errors, identify the best opportunities, and find the results.)

Government. With its great benefits, expanding scope and budget (not only federal but state and local as well), and a pretty good record avoiding discrimination, it's hard to beat the opportunities available through the government. Of special interest are the opportunities available at the Internal Revenue Service, the U.S. Small Business Association, and the Peace Corps. These three federal agencies have expressed particular interest in hiring experienced older workers; however, you can find this same interest at most government bureaus. This also applies at many places that you think of as a young man's game, such as police departments, the airport, and public recreation facilities.

RELATIVE DIFFICULTY OF CHANGING CAREERS

Before you decide if you're going to actually change careers—take extra caution. Sometimes we feel like we want to change careers when the real thing we need a change from isn't our career itself but something about our last position (a poor manager, a bad company culture, etc.). Changing careers—though exhilarating and worth it—can also be very, very difficult. Look at the chart below to see the relative ease or difficulty associated with a change in careers. (The higher the number, the greater the difficulty.)

PULLING AN INSIDE JOB

Many of those unadvertised jobs go to people who already work inside of the company. And, if you think about it, that certainly makes sense. Hiring an existing employee takes a lot of the risk out of the hiring process. The company will already know many of the factors that make or break

1	2	5
Same Job	Same Job	Same Job
Same Industry	Similar Industry	Different Industry
3	**4**	**7**
Similar Job	Similar Job	Similar Job
Same Industry	Similar Industry	Different Industry
6	**8**	**9**
Different Job	Different Job	Different Job
Same Industry	Similar Industry	Different Industry

a good employee/employer relationship. Many of these questions will already have been answered:

- Is he going to be on time? Absent a lot?
- Does she get along with her coworkers? Does she "fit in" around here?
- Can I trust him?
- Does she take directions well?

Now, if being referred for a position gives you a 42 times advantage over candidates not referred, *what kind of number do you think we're looking at for internal candidates compared to external candidates?*

So, what is the method? Simply get a job—any job—at a company that offers you an opportunity to move into the desired career or department. For instance, let's say you are currently an accountant but you would like to change careers and become a marketing director. It is difficult to change careers, especially in time of heavy unemployment. There are just too many unknowns about you, added to the fact that you have no marketing experience. You start out with two strikes right off the bat.

But if you identify a company that has a progressive marketing department, it would serve your long-term career well by getting a job in the accounting department (or actually a job anywhere within the company). Work hard, produce impressive results, and earn a reputation for being an outstanding employee. Get to know all the department heads, especially those in the targeted department. Have lunch with them. Find ways to be of service. Attend meetings they attend—such as volunteer CPR classes or the president's state-of-the-company address. Also, use this time to pick up any needed skills or education (and the company will probably pay for it!).

Eventually you will hear of an opening in the targeted department. Before the job is ever even posted for internal employees, your grapevine will probably sense the opportunity. Gather support from friends you have made in the department, approach the person you would be reporting to, and . . .

Yes, this works. It is especially strong for those wanting to shift careers, but works equally well if you want to keep your career but move up the ladder.

But there are some disadvantages:

- Assuming you have to take a pay cut initially, can your family survive?
- Waiting for an opening takes time, possibly a couple of years. Again, will the income be sufficient during the interim?

- To make this approach worthwhile, make sure you want to make a career shift and your family is willing to make the needed sacrifice. Remember, it could be a career disaster if you follow this method and change your mind in midstream, but maybe not. The worst that could happen is that you are stuck in a good company in which you have a lot of friends, good connections, and a great reputation.

If you don't like competition, or hate the activities needed for an aggressive job search, this is the method for you.

YOUR RESUME

Before we leave the topic of seeking other employment, let's do a basic primer on your resume. This document is the most overrated part of a job search, yet it is also your most underrated. Let me explain. There is a myth out there that a great resume will get you a job. No unqualified person has ever gotten a job because of a great resume. True, a well-written resume can frame you in such a way that a hiring manager may want to interview you, but no words can overcome shallow credentials.

On the other hand, care should be taken to write a good resume. After all, it is the only piece of paper that is certain to go into your employment file. (Future promotions involving a transfer to another department may begin with another department head flipping through your file.) And there is a tremendous amount that you can learn about yourself by putting forth the work required to create a credible document.

There are many ways to build a good resume but for the sake of simplicity I'll just show you one. The format is clean, easy to read, and enables you to show you at your best. It is also "age friendly." While not hiding your age, it does de-emphasize it while not diminishing your experience. Let's look at the various parts of this resume and discuss the elements used to make it effective for you.

Type

There are three types of resumes: chronological, functional, and combined. Professional HR people prefer the chronological because it clearly shows the jobs you had and highlights any gaps. Red flags really stand out in a chronological resume, often making it a document that works against you instead of for you. Also age is not only apparent, it is broadcast loudly.

A functional resume focuses on skills rather than job titles and dates. While it does an excellent job hiding red flags and is great for career changes, HR recruiters are suspicious of them. They know that a functional resume can hide red flags so they immediately become suspicious and dig deep hoping to catch the dirt.

But then there is the combined resume. The combined resume does just that, combine the best of the functional resume with the best of the chronological. Notice that while it lists all the information the recruiter needs, it just doesn't highlight dates and terms that emphasize your age. But also, just like a functional resume, it does highlight your skills, talents, and abilities. These attributes make the combined resume excellent for career changes.

How Many Pages?

After many years of championing the one-page resume, most HR gurus are backing off a bit. Here is a good way to look at it: one page is great if you can do so while also listing your accomplishments. And, one-page resumes work if you are early in your career. But since the readers of this book are not early in their careers, I now recommend you extend it to two pages, as the example in this chapter indicates. Two pages gives you plenty of room to include your credentials and accomplishments without being tempted to use mice-type font sizes or quarter-inch margins. Three pages should be a rarity; however some educational, medical, and scientific resumes traditionally contain lists that require such length.

Recruiters tell us that they spend an average of 16 seconds in the initial resume screening; organize your sections clearly so that he or she will have no trouble finding those areas they feel are most critical.

Technical Setup

Here are a few pointers on the technical setup.

- Use easy-to-read typefaces such as Arial or Times New Roman. Avoid fonts that draw attention to themselves.
- Use 11- or 12-point type for the text. Smaller font sizes will be difficult for some to read and may blur when copied.
- Use a high-quality linen or cotton paper to emphasize your professionalism. Also, there is a good chance that you haven't looked for a job in over 15 years. You may remember in those days it was popular to print your resume on tinted paper (blue, gray, and tan were the most popular). That's no longer the case. Colored paper is just not taken seriously. Use white paper. Besides looking current, it also photocopies best.
- Black ink only. Emphasize words with bold or italics, never colors.
- Remember this is an advertisement, not a biography. Keep it concise. Less is more. ("Yes, but if less is more, think how much more *more* would be," Dr. Frasier Crane)

The Heading

Your name should be listed as you are referred to every day in the workplace. If your legal name is Samuel Douglas Roberts, III, list it as simply Sam Roberts, if that's what your coworkers call you. The long formal name can look a bit too pompous and that's not the impression you want to project. There is a limit to the informality, however. Don't list a nickname. Bubba, Junior, and Dawg have no place on the resume. (Or really in your life, once you reach the age of 12.)

List one telephone number where you can be reached. Things get too complex when you list home, office, and cell. Besides, home and office numbers run too many risks—the caller may reach your children or your boss. It's best just to list your cell; you can control the message and it's pretty much always with you.

Also, list your e-mail address. I recommend you get a separate account just for your job search. (*Never* use your office email.) Free addresses are available from several sources. I recommend yahoo.com, mail.com, or Google's Gmail. As with names, keep your email address businesslike. You would be surprised at some of the address I have seen on resumes. Some of them create red flags in the recruiter's mind right off the bat. Not a good first impression. And if possible, try to get an address that is your name. For instance, my address is a very workable kentanner@consultant.com.

The Profile

Create a short statement, about 50 words that summarizes your experience, skills, and abilities that you can bring to the company. I realize this is easier said than done, in fact for most folks it's the toughest part of the resume. Start by simply making a list of the traits you want to include, then turn them into good declaratory sentences. Don't be afraid to ask friends for help on this or even your kid's English teacher. The profile sets the tone for the resume and you don't want to begin weakly.

Skill Summary

List four to six specific skills that you excel at. At a glance, the recruiter will know your strong points and be able to shape your credentials. This actually serves as a framework for the rest of the resume. Where do you get the bullet points for the skill summary? From the next section, "Selected Accomplishments." (Hey, I never said that a resume was written in order.) Review your accomplishments and you will begin to see themes. You may have several that could be summarized as "leadership" for instance, so that becomes an important bullet point. Strive to have the skill summary points tied to the accomplishments. That way when the interviewer says, "It says here that you excel at communications," you can reply, "Yes. If you look below at the accomplishments section I give three examples of that . . ." and then you proceed to discuss all the wonderful things you have done in communications.

Selected Accomplishments

This is one of the many uses of the exercise I put you through in chapter 4. Besides being a wonderful motivator and tool for discovering your career direction, the accomplishments exercise is a great tool for building your resume. Pick 6 to 10 off of your list. Use not only those that are most impressive but those that fit well for the job you are seeking.

Here's what I mean by that. You should shape your resume to fit each job you apply for. Different jobs require slightly different skills, so pick from your long list of accomplishments those that best represent the things you can do for each separate employer.

Experience

You may notice that this section makes up the entirety of most resumes. Too many people think of a resume as just a list of companies, titles, and dates. That is a shame, but at least you can celebrate that that is what your competition is settling for. A good resume frames your past experience so that it shows career progression. While you want to show dates, you don't want to highlight them. To do this, list dates all the way to the right instead of in the highly visible left margin.

Another way to de-emphasize age is by only going back three jobs or 15 years, whichever seems most appropriate. If you feel you need to list more jobs, try summarizing them in one short paragraph as shown.

Education

List degrees in reverse order along with the colleges attended and dates of graduation. Yes, always put the dates. They are expected and if omitted the recruiter will assume there is a reason. Also list any degrees in progress, major coursework, or certifications in this section.

If you do not have a degree, it's OK to list courses taken or schools attended, just as long as you don't phrase it in such a way that the reader would infer a degree. Many recruiters would consider such behavior as a knockout. Also, if there is no degree, you might group all your education and certifications with the next category and call it Education/Other.

SAM ROBERTS

1440 Westclover Circle

Kennesaw, GA 30072

678.555.1212

samroberts@email.com

Profile

An energetic and creative leader with broad experience in management, construction, and development, as well as in training, who has proven himself by working through the ranks to attain regional general management positions. The collection of experiences has lead to an expertise in:

- **Operations**
- **People Development**
- **Site Development**
- **Management**
- **Construction**
- **Training**

Selected Accomplishments

- Citizen of the Year, North Cobb County, 2005.
- Decreased turnover 50%–90% in every assignment held.
- Opened 18 stores and 47 restaurants, all delivered on time and under budget.
- Recognized as a developer of people, credited for helping 18 subordinates be promoted while serving in his department or organization.
- Developed chain-wide marketing program that increased quarterly sales 18%.
- Winner of President's Innovation Award, *Roundabout Burgers*, 1992.
- President's Award for department innovations, *The Picture Show*, 2007.
- Designed and executed $25,000,000 remodeling project for pizza chain that increased customer count by 9% nationwide.
- Written seven published articles about innovations in retail construction.
- Implemented changes saving over $48,000 per unit in construction costs.
- Worked full time through college, completely paying for education through scholarships and money earned.

Experience

The Picture Show, LLC   Atlanta, GA   1998–2009

Regional Vice President of Operations, 2002–2009

Oversaw operations of six-state region composed of 160 movie rental stores.

District Manager, 1998–2002

Oversaw twelve stores in Atlanta area

Promenade Pizza Corp. Nashville, TN   1992–1998

Manager of Construction and Development

Found promising locations, negotiated financing, and supervised construction of new restaurants for this regional pizza chain.

Roundabout Burger Corporation   Memphis, TN   1981–1992

Director of Real Estate, 1987–1992

Area Operations Director, 1981–1987

Worked through the ranks from operations to become key staff executive.

Previous positions include area supervisor with Burger King Corp and accounting positions with Danver's and Subway. (1977–1981)

Education

Masters of Business Administration

Georgia State University, 1992

Atlanta, GA

Bachelors of Business Administration in Accounting

University of Memphis, 1977

Memphis, TN

Attended numerous marketing, management, and leadership courses at *Columbia University, Stanford University,* and the *University of Chicago*

Personal/Other

- Past-President of Cobb County Jaycees
- Citizen of the Year, North Cobb County, 2005
- Made a "Tennessee Colonel" by the governor, 1998
- Enjoys travel, playing softball, and watching University of Memphis basketball

Available for heavy travel and relocation

Personal/Other

Most counselors will disagree with the advice I am about to give. They will tell you that personal information has no place on a resume; it should be all business. But what if that personal information helps you get a job? It often does and that is why I like to list it.

Here is a good example. As you know, it is illegal for the interviewer to ask you about marital status or children. But there is nothing illegal about you telling her. Suppose you are applying for a job in which personal stability would be impressive to the company. Don't you think "married 23 years with three teenage children" might score a few points? Also, the fact is that so much of the hiring decision is based on whether the interviewer likes you or not. (I'm not defending this, just stating the facts.) It's always good to have some way to connect with the interviewer such as hobbies you both enjoy. Listing personal information gives you the opportunity to connect with an interview and, at the very least, furnishes a conversation starter for those awkward first few minutes.

Be careful not to list controversial groups or even names of specific organizations. "Active in church" is just great but you take a risk naming the exact denomination. I was once executive secretary for a group advocating stricter gun controls, but this being Georgia I decided to summarize it as "officer in political action group." Use good discretion in your listings but put any information on your resume that might help build your image or help you bond with the people hiring you.

YES, IT'S GOOD ENOUGH. MOVE ON

No matter how brilliant of a job you do constructing your resume, there will always be a temptation to tweak it a bit more. So you'll pull it up on your computer and try to think of some better action verbs. Then you'll play with the fonts a bit and think of a couple of nouveau-adjectives for the Profile section. Pretty soon you'll look up and it's 11 o'clock; time to fix a bite of lunch.

There are several high-quality time wasters you will face in a job search. Tweaking the resume is one. Internet job boards are another. You will get engrossed in the activity, kidding yourself that you are working hard at your job search, when all that's really happening is you are having call reluctance and avoiding picking up the phone. (Hey, I'm not criticizing. I'm the world champion at this. Several times while writing this book I convinced myself that it was more important that I turn on C-SPAN and watch the Senate agriculture subcommittee's hearing on wheat subsidies in southwest Idaho.)

Once you have produced a darn good resume, stop. Move on. The time expended to slightly improve a good resume could be put to much better use elsewhere—such as watching ESPN's coverage of the Abe Lincoln Memorial Log Splitting Contest.

Avoid clichés like the plague. Never put on a resume "excellent health" or "references available upon request." These things are assumed and are just tired, old-fashioned space fillers. On the other hand, here is a tagline that will score you big points. If it is true, end your resume with "available for heavy travel and relocation." These days most people are not interested in travel and refuse to relocate. Having either one of those flexibilities will definitely set you apart from the competition.

THE INTERVIEW

There was a fine discussion of interviewing in chapter two, but it focused purely on dealing with age discrimination. The days of walking into the employment office and filling out an application are long gone. In fact, interviewing is quite a production these days. Interviewers now expect you to already know a great deal about their organization. They want active participation including your asking lots of intelligent targeted questions. They rarely accept yes or no answers, instead they seek lots of examples and stories to back up your facts. Let's look at some of these interview elements and study how you can do an impressive job.

Preparing for the Interviews

Immediately begin preparing for the interview the moment you decide to apply to a specific company. Your biggest task to learn all you can about that company. What's to learn? Here's a list to begin with:

- products and/or services
- global footprint/emerging markets
- recent or pending M&A activity to predict cultural shifting
- recent press releases
- stock price over last 3–5 years (look for spikes, dips, trending)
- executive board members and senior leadership team for current alliances and previous cultural mindsets
- current economic impact on business
- Their competitors and percentage of market share they possess.
- know the names, titles, and reporting structure of the interviewers to understand their perspective and how you can help them accomplish their objectives

That's a pretty hefty assignment and it might take you a while to find all this out, but doing so will greatly enhance your chances for a successful interview.

The Screening Interview

Here is something that may surprise you. The purpose of the screening interview (usually held over the phone) is to determine if you are qualified for the job. Now your immediate thought might be, I thought that was the purpose of the entire process! If the screening interview is to determine your qualifications, what is the personal interview for? I'll keep you in suspense for a few paragraphs on that one; first, we'll cover some tips for getting past the screener.

Prepare yourself thoroughly for this interview. Many people make the mistake of assuming that it is just a formality before the real interview takes place. Know what the company really wants by reviewing their Web site; talking with employees or former employees if possible; and talking to colleagues who may be familiar with aspects of the company culture.

The screening interview is usually held over the phone. In a large company, a junior person in the HR department—possibly even an intern—usually does this interview. That is because most questions are rather cut-and-dried; the answers really don't need a lot of interpreting. The interviewer often has a checklist of the job qualifications that may have been stated in the job posting. Therefore, it is important that you be prepared for this line of questioning. Have your list ready, correlating your qualifications with their requirements. Have examples for each.

If you do not have one of the stated qualifications, be prepared to address the deficiency. Have several other qualities or experiences that can make up for any item missing. For example:

They ask for:	Here is what you have:
10 years experience	8 years of successful experience
MBA	BBA, plus headed a nationally recognized product rollout delivering $12,000,000 in profit
expertise as a plaintiff's attorney	expertise as a defense attorney and can bring 12 corporate clients with you

Be prepared to give examples and evidence of your credentials, both tangible credentials (10 years experience) and intangible qualities (leadership, personable, hard worker, etc.). Keep your answers short. Thirty seconds is good, never more that a minute. If they want more information, they will ask for it. Be aware that the interviewer will be trained to zero in on any holes in your resume. Be prepared to address obvious red flags, such as employment gaps, missing qualifications, or suspicious items left unaddressed.

Be respectful of the phone screen interviewer. Even if she doesn't rank very high in the company's hierarchy, for the next few minutes she holds your future in her hands. They are the gatekeeper, and you must endear yourself to that person, as if she was the hiring manager. Don't become frustrated if you find the screening interviewer not as savvy on business terms as you are (acronyms, technical knowledge, professional associations, and competition in the industry). Instead use it as an opportunity to share your knowledge, patience, and communication skills. Educate the interviewer in a professional manner. They will appreciate the way you dealt with them.

Never interrupt the interviewer, ever. Not only is it impolite, but you may miss some important information. Take notes during your screening interview. Ask for a brief description of what the job is at the beginning of the interview and take notes on the key points made by the interviewer. Use these notes to reference in your wrap up of the interview—hitting your experience relative to their needs in the organization.

First Impressions

Remember that your interview begins the minute you pull onto the parking lot. Horror stories abound of people being rude to someone in the parking lot who ended up being the very person they later interviewed with. So much of our image is developed during those times when we think no one is looking. That is particularly true while in the waiting room. Here are some points you might find trite but let me assure you that when it comes to projecting an image, your first impression is not trite.

- Walk in with a smile on your face. Approach the receptionist confidently. Wait patiently if she is on the phone or talking with someone else, and greet her in a friendly manner.
- Decline any offers of coffee or anything else to drink. This is not a matter of courtesy, but it's just that drinks are awkward to handle between the waiting room and the office.
- If you must read something, pick up company literature instead of *People* magazine.
- Sit so that it is easy to stand up. Avoid the deep, padded chairs, as they are awkward to get out of. Not a good first image.
- Be on your best behavior. You would be surprised how many people blow any chance of employment by being rude to the receptionist.

YOU WILL THANK ME FOR THESE SECRET WEAPONS

Here are two tips that could be the very things that lead to getting the job offer. Do I have your attention now? Thought so. Use these techniques on the next cycle of interviews, one for the beginning and one at the end.

Beginning: When it appears that the initial small talk is over and the "Q&A" is about to begin, ask this question, "What was it about my credentials or background that led to your inviting me here today?" The interviewer will almost certainly respond with a thorough answer, getting the interview off to a positive beginning. (He's complimenting you right off the bat!) But more importantly, the interviewer is also telling you what is important to him. Make note of these things and prepare extensive examples to emphasize the very issues he has told you are most important.

End: Have you ever had a great interview and then, as you were driving away, recalled an answer you gave or comment made that you sure wish you could take back? You would like to redo the moment, but because of that space-time continuum thingie, you figured you would just have to live with it. I have good news for you. You get a second chance.

Write a thank you note as soon as you get home. In that note, include a paragraph that starts something like this, "I've been thinking about our discussion of management styles, and I thought it important to mention how I am a big believer in *Management By Wandering Around*. Here are some important results I've had . . ." and then go on to craft a brilliant discussion on the subject. The end result? The future boss will forget your original dumb answer since you have now overshadowed it with brilliance. You have replaced your weakest part of the interview with your strongest message. Now *that* will bring your grade point average up.

Beginning the Interview

Let me tell you my best advice for how to approach an interview. Use all the skills you have to turn the interview from a question-and-answer session into a conversation. Q&A is too formal and stiff for either of you to really get to know each other. A good business discussion does allow everyone to get their questions answered and learn a great deal about each other, but does so in a more relaxed, non-BS manner than a Q&A format. How do you get a good business conversation going? It's tough, but you may have success in how you answer the initial questions. Begin by briefly staying off business. Comment on office décor or have a story about the Notre Dame pennant hanging on his wall. Quickly find some common ground to create a bond. Another way is in your answer to her "questions." If you give clichéd answers, you'll never get into a conversation. Also, look at your language and demeanor. Try to parrot the interviewer's posture and general demeanor.

Answering the Questions

Ah, this has been the part you've been waiting for, isn't it? You are looking for all the magic answers to the trick questions they will ask. You memorize those and voila! You are hired. Guess what? That's not going to happen mainly because memorized clichéd answers usually strike out.

So, instead of the memorization method—the interviewer asks you questions that he read from the book *1,000 Great Interview Questions!* and you answer these questions using what you memorized from the book *1,000 Great Answers to Interview Questions!*—seems to me that it would be so much more time efficient if the two of you would just swap books and skip the dialog. Here's a few pointers that will make the process flow a bit better for you.

First, be prepared to speak to your accomplishments. Use stories of your experiences and mountains you have conquered to answer his questions and back up claims you will make. Where do we get these accomplishments? That's right, this is one more use of the exercise performed in chapter 5. Look through that long list of accomplishments and label each one with the skills (plural) it demonstrates. Group similar skills together and make sure you have accomplishments included for all the things the interviewer is certain to ask you about. This is your key to acing the interview. While others are just claiming to be good leaders, you can give three solid examples.

The Three "Likes" of Interviewing

So, if they determined that you are qualified during the screening interview, what are they trying to find out with the personal interviews? The company, whether they realize it or not, wants to find out about three "likes": Do we like her? Does she like us? Is she like the rest of us?

"Do We Like Her?"

Here is a scary thought. Most of the interviewers' hiring decision consists of information gathered in the first 90 seconds. Realize that is during the "smalltalk" phase; you have not had time to answer any questions yet. Things like how you are dressed, your handshake, your confidence, and your smile seem to carry more weight than your brilliant analysis of projected Saudi Arabian oil reserves.

Learn how to excel at the "smalltalk" game. Look around the office for clues as to the interviewers' interests and business demeanor. (There is a big difference in business demeanor between someone who decorates their office with pictures of family and college sports memorabilia versus a wall-full of charts and graphs.) The key here is to bond with the interviewer. You want to be "liked" by whatever definition the interviewer has in mind.

"Does She Like Us?"

Everyone wants to be liked. Especially when you work around them 40 hours a week. Communicate through body language and through your answers that you enjoy being in this office and genuinely like the people. (Especially the interviewer.) Avoid the obvious comments, but certainly make everyone you come in contact feel liked. Don't be afraid to blatantly say at some point, "I don't know what it is about this place, but I really like the people here."

"Is She Like Us?"

Here is what the interviewer is thinking. *Will she fit in with this company? Is this a culture match? Everyone else around here comes in early and stays late. Will she? Will she get along with everyone around here or is she stuck-up?* Observe the people in the office and comments made at the interview for clues to company culture. Find a way to work into the conversation way that you match what you see. Then again, the interview is a two-way street. If you see a culture you cannot live with, figure that into your decision as to whether to accept any job offer they may make.

Asking the Questions

As I mentioned earlier, you will be expected to carry your own in this interview/discussion. Failure to ask questions makes you look like a desperate applicant, not an executive who has some choices. But failure to ask questions is not the biggest sin. The biggest sin would be asking questions that are shallow or nonsubstantive. For example, "How's business?" or "How much time do we get for lunch?" show you haven't put much thought into the interview. Asking questions that can be answered just by glancing at the Web site also shows a lack of interest. Here are some examples of productive questions to ask:

- I noticed on your Web site that you are rolling out a new line of shampoos. What needs did you see in the marketplace that prompted that?
- One of the things that attracted me to this company is that you seem to be weathering the economy quite nicely while the rest of the industry is suffering. What's your secret?

- You seem to be having a successful career here. What do you most enjoy about working for this company?

And go ahead and ask some questions specifically about your candidacy.

- What would a successful candidate for this job look like?
- Do you have any concerns about my ability to do this job?

Use his answers to help shape a "closing statement" for the interview, clearing up any unresolved matters or framing your qualifications around the qualifications he mentioned.

SHOULD YOU ACCEPT THE JOB?

If you've been wandering in the woods and have eaten nothing for days, even a handful of snails, raw fish, and some mysterious mushrooms will look like a gourmet meal. It works the same way when experiencing a long drought of joblessness. That Walmart greeter job begins to look like it just might stimulate you intellectually. Or the automotive stock futures broker job really will pay the bills if you talk to enough of your old college frat buddies. Or the Commodore 64 computer repair shop really does seem to have a fine future.

When times are scary, we tend to convince ourselves that longshots will indeed come through. And when you are at that point, it is awfully tempting to take any job that comes along. While doing so may take a big load off your back initially, the weight rapidly returns as you face the reality that this may not be the right job for you. Worse yet, if you pick the wrong job there is a probability that within six months you'll be right back in the same situation you started with. And instead of dining on escargot, sushi, and mushrooms, you are back to eating snails, raw fish, and toadstools. Put the job through one final test before accepting. Ask yourself these five questions.

"Do You Fit in with the Company's Culture?"

You will be spending more of your waking hours with the people at this company than you will with your family. Does the workplace offer a culture that you want to be a part of? Don't approach it like some approach their future husband (yes, he has some issues, but I'll change him). You cannot change a company's culture unless you are the top guy, and even then, change comes only after a lot of painful headbanging.

"Do You Like the People There?"

Once again, you'll be spending more time with the company's employees than with your family. While you don't need a warm, loving relationship with your coworkers, you do need to be able to function pleasantly. I have seen a candidate reject a high-paying, high-potential job in sales at a Christian radio station because he couldn't stand being around "all those Jesus freaks." It's okay if others come from a different lifestyle or belief system, but if you don't respect their beliefs—or if you actually resent them—you'll have problems. In this case, the salesman made a good choice.

"What Happened to the Last Person?"

Ask the interviewer what happened to the last guy. Do some more digging if he implies that the position has seen a lot of turnover. Talk to some of the employees and find out if there is a lot of turnover in general. Explore the boss more deeply, take another look at the job objectives and goals. Turnover, especially in this economy, doesn't occur for no reason. Make sure the job really is what you think it is.

"Is Compensation Appropriate?"

The answer to this question actually involves two different topics. No matter how the company justifies the compensation package, you must decline if it does not meet your needs. If they offer no health plan and you have a disabled child, you must decline. If the salary does not approach what you need to maintain your acceptable standard of living, you must decline. What about accepting it until you find something better? Possibly, but that rarely works. Most full-time positions leave you inadequate time to pursue other work, plus you'll feel guilty doing that.

The other reason to decline a low salary is if it does not reflect a realistically reflect your real value to them. If the offer is just a bit low, play the game and negotiate it back in the ballpark. But if it is just plain silly—you expected $100,000 and they offered $65,000—you need to have one last short conversation. Explain to them that you thoroughly researched the market and what similar companies pay for positions of this level. Your research showed a range of $95,000 to $110,000. Give him an opportunity to prove you wrong or to make a dramatic adjustment in the offer, but realize that there is no way you can negotiate an offer up by 54 percent. Not only is his offer inadequate for your needs, but also shows the company does not understand or value the position it is trying to fill.

Also, let's address the opposite extreme. Don't accept a position just because the pay is huge. True, an unusually large compensation will cover a multitude of minor issues, but if just about all the job has going for it is a big paycheck, then I urge you to swallow hard and then do the courageous thing—pass on the job. No money will cover 50 hours of misery a week.

"Is This the Best Offer I Will Probably Get?"

It is easy to talk yourself into any situation when the alligators are snapping at your heels. In fact, if this is the only offer you can see on the horizon, it is natural to be blind to what might normally be obvious downsides. Do find a moment to honestly reflect. Will this job further my career? Is this job pretty much what I was hoping for when I started my search? Is there a reasonable possibility that another, better position might become available on my timetable?

Now don't make the same mistake in the opposite direction, either. Look, there is no magic available in making this decision. Just don't fall into either trap, taking a job out of desperation or rejecting a job because it's not perfect. If you are currently employed then you absolutely should hold out for that perfect job. If you are not employed and it is a good opportunity that fits your needs reasonably well, take it.

A COMPLETE SOLUTION

Here is a way to have your cake and eat it too. Temp agencies and staffing firms are placing far more than just typists, secretaries, receptionists, and administrative staff these days. They also deal in placing accountants, attorneys, and even senior management. Temping will give you some cash flow while you explore different jobs, careers, and companies. And, if you find a company you like, use the strategies previously discussed to pull an inside job. Temping is a great way to get to know the company and for them to get to know you.

Part III

The Top of the Pyramid

Roger reached that point in his life in which he began focusing his energies on the pursuit of self-actualization. He retired from his job as a bricklayer and formed his own company, dedicated to the creation of a machine that would create energy without using any. Yes, Roger was going to build a perpetual motion machine.

Roger went though hundreds of unsuccessful prototypes until he had his Eureka moment. He was eating a jelly sandwich when his cat walked into the lab. It was then that he recalled two absolute laws of nature. One was that a cat always lands on its feet. The other was that a jelly sandwich always lands jelly-side down. Roger grabbed the cat and strapped a jelly sandwich to its back. He dropped the jelly cat, which stopped in mid-air three feet above the floor and began spinning, faster and faster until it reached the ideal speed for energy generation.

There will be a point in your career where you, like Roger, are able to drop most other pursuits and focus on the attainment of goals much higher than yourself. You might do this by starting a business, volunteering, or just pursuing a life of travel. Whatever your choice, your career is now focused not so much on the money it generates but the self-satisfaction it creates. The last third of this book is dedicated to that pursuit of self-actualization.

You may be wondering what happened to Roger's jelly cat. Roger learned patents are not issued for perpetual motion machines; however, it is reported that agents from the Trilateral Commission broke in to Roger's lab, stole the jelly cat, and are now holding it at Area 51. Why? I don't know. Perhaps the only way we'll ever find out is if Will Smith makes another movie.

Chapter 9

Independence Day

CREATING YOUR OWN COMPANY

Owning your own business has always been considered an important part of the American dream. It has the image of prestige, freedom, and success. Being your own boss is also seen as the ultimate in personal security. While that statement is not true if you define security as guaranteed success, it is true in another way. You are completely accountable for your destiny. If you fail, it's your fault. If you succeed, it's completely to your credit. Whatever label you place on the business becomes attached to you.

There is no better time to consider owning your own business than middle age or retirement. You have built a lifetime of experience, you are at the apex of your career, and you have (hopefully) built an impressive network of advisors and friends.

Look in the Mirror

There are no guarantees in business, and you can't eliminate all the risks with going into business. Before quitting your job or investing your life savings, ponder these questions.

Are You Doing It for the Right Reasons? Let me tell you the wrong reason. Don't go into business for yourself just because you want to be your own boss (especially if the urge hit you right after having a fight with your boss). Look, right now you have one boss. When you are in business for yourself, you'll have dozens. You'll have to answer to the bank, your family, suppliers, the franchise group, and—most of all—customers. Sometimes they'll be good reasonable people, just like most bosses. But you can be assured that there will be enough screamers and schemers that you will experience headaches that'll make you wish you were back in the cold embrace of Ebenezer Scrooge.

Do You Have the Money? A clichéd rule of thumb is that everything takes twice as long and costs twice as much. That is probably not a formal accounting formula, but I imagine most financial advisors agree with it. Don't let the excitement of owning a business deceive you into underestimating the need for adequate funding.

Do You Have Experience in this Particular Business? Too many people enter a business assuming that they will pick up the tricks of the trade. If the trade is similar to yours, perhaps. But dramatically different businesses will be tough, if not impossible, to learn while running the business. For instance, accountants shouldn't open a restaurant unassisted. One way around this may be to purchase a franchise. We'll explore that option later in the chapter.

How Will You Handle the Lost Benefits? One powerful pull that keeps you at your current job are the benefits, particularly health insurance.

Have You Addressed Any Missing Skills? If your career has been based on running part of a business, such as marketing, purchasing, or sales, you may need to pick up skills that are missing in your personal inventory. This can be addressed by taking the right courses at a local college, hiring experts to help, or bringing in a partner, but make sure you have taken the necessary steps to cover the areas you lack.

Are You Really a Self-starter? If you have spent a few decades peacefully going home at five knowing that if any problems pop up someone else would handle it, or if you are simply used to going home at five every day, then the lifestyle shock of owning a business might be overwhelming. Do you really want to take on the around-the-clock aspect of business ownership? What about the long hours and the final accountability? Can you handle seven 12-hour workdays every week?

Do You Like Making Decisions? You will not only have to make all the decisions, but you will do so without a safety net. There will be no boss or support department to catch your mistakes. Some people are terrified of this prospect, others revel in the independence.

And Most Important . . . How will the business affect your family? A new business will have a dramatic effect on your family, especially during the first few years. Are they prepared for the lowered standard of living? Can everyone deal with the change in lifestyle due to the long hours you will be working? Have you discussed the possibilities of family members needing to work in the business?

You may feel a bit depressed while reviewing this list. That may be because I intentionally phrased much of it quite negatively. But there is a reason for this. Too many people jump into this major life change with

A WORD ABOUT RISK

I tell the Michael Jordan story (see chapter 8) at just about every career seminar I hold. Invariably, someone will come up to me afterward to share their own story about MJ. Here is a popular one: "Do you know why Michael Jordan is so successful? It's because he isn't afraid of failure. He'll take risks just so he can earn the successes."

Now that's a pretty inspirational story but it has one small flaw. The fact is I would also be willing to take a whole boatload of risks if—just like Mike—I had half a billion dollars in my checking account.

Risk carries a lot of risk with it. By now you have decided what your level of risk tolerance is, but I urge you to take another look at it. I took a lot of risks when I was younger, knowing that I had plenty of time to recover from failure. I'm still open to a lot more risk than most folks, but admit I'm considerably more conservative in my definition of "reasonable." Make certain you can accept the consequences of the risk you take on at this stage in your life.

little consideration of the very real monsters lurking. Too many people flop into financial ruin because they failed to ask the important questions. But here is the good news. If you worked your way through these issues and were able to address each of them fully and positively, then there's a good chance you are ready to make the leap.

STARTING THE BUSINESS

Once you have make the decision to start you business, the real fun begins. Once again, a lot of critical decisions must be made. Before doing anything else, write a business plan. This is not just a feel-good exercise. Writing a business plan forces you to do the research you must do in order to put together a successful venture. You'll explore the market for your products, competition, budgets and financing, and personnel needs. You will see how much money you'll need, ask questions about your abilities, and learn of the biggest challenges you will face. The business plan will not only become your roadmap for operating your new business, it may very well point out that maybe you should not go into this business, saving you from potential career and financial disaster. Do not go into business until you have a great business plan.

First you must make a most basic decision: what kind of business should I start? Here are two great pieces of advice to help you decide. The first is this: *Do what you love.* You will be spending more time with your business than with your family; you cannot afford to spend those hours trudging through tasks that bore you. The ultimate success of your business depends on this too. The fact is we usually excel at projects we enjoy and rarely succeed with things we dislike. It's important that you truly enjoy what you do, whether it be building canoes, creating pottery, or decorating homes.

The other jewel of wisdom is the most basic piece of advice ever given on selecting a business: *Find a need and fill it.* Yes, this sentence has reached cliché status, but the reason ideas become clichés is by being right. The easiest business to run is one that produces products or services that people already know they need. That way you don't have to spend time and money convincing people they need what you have. Instead you can concentrate on explaining why your product is their best value for scratching their itch.

If at all possible, start your business while you are still employed. The early stages of a business's life are long on expenses and short on cash, regardless of financing you have secured or savings you have accumulated. Having the security of a paycheck and benefits will go a long way in allowing you to begin your new life panic-free. Plus, it will give you an immediate fallback should you discover you made the wrong choice in the selection of your new business.

How long do you stay before taking the plunge? Get things set up and on solid ground. For instance, get some customers lined up. Do the networking; select your suppliers and product design. Sell or even give away your products or services. You can't start marketing too soon.

Also, get your money lined up. The days have long passed where you could write a brilliant business plan and then walk into a bank and expect them to hand you money. It never really worked that way and certainly doesn't today. Traditional lenders don't like businesses that don't have a proven track record. So, verify the amount of cash you can put into your venture and identify potential investors. Develop your budget, and price potential suppliers. Make certain you will have the cash available to support the early lean times.

Build a team. Even if you are going to be a one-person shop, surround yourself with advisors. I know a very successful entrepreneur who builds a board of advisors for each business he starts. He'll get people well known in the industry to serve on the board at no salary. Once a quarter he'll buy them dinner, toss out some issues he is working on, and listen to their advice. Besides getting all this incredible consulting for free, he finds these advisors quite useful in networking to new clients. But don't limit your support system to a formal board. Find a mentor and other businesspeople that you can toss ideas around over a cup of coffee. Make use of free government programs such as the Service Corps of Retired Executives or the Small Business Association. With not much effort, you can build an executive committee that would rival large corporations.

Be active in your industry associations. Yes, these are your competitors but they can be your best friends. Besides, industry associations usually offer a plethora of seminars, group purchasing power, and networking opportunities.

Consulting

To diminish risk, get into a business that requires little cash to start up and maintain. Starting a retail store? A restaurant? Product manufacturing? You better have a lot of cash. And if the venture fails (this is a possibility you cannot ignore), you risk losing hundreds of thousands—perhaps millions—of dollars. But if you begin a one-man shop such as a consulting business, you need very little cash. You can operate out of your home, use existing business and office equipment. If you have a phone, a computer, and business cards, you can hang out your shingle. Another huge benefit of not needing a lot of cash to begin is that the early, lean times are easier to survive. Rather than the constant pressure of making rent money or payroll, you can focus on your core business. And, if the worst comes and you can't seem to make the business work, you have little to risk. Recovery is quick as you await your next big idea.

Companies, even in good times, are constantly in the habit of downsizing. It is considered good management to downsize, rightsize, regroup, and reconfigure. Even though they are gaining huge efficiencies by throwing people out the door, the fact remains that they still need to do all the work these ex-employees formerly did. More and more companies are outsourcing for the services and expertise no longer available from their own staff. Despite the growing need, establishing a consulting practice is not easy. Consulting is a constant process of securing clients and solving their problems. Strong expertise and solid reputation do not guarantee success. Never make the mistake of believing that your reputation can sell itself you can simply sit and wait for work. Half of your work hours could easily be spent just looking for work.

That is why it is important that you get that first big client. This may be easier than it first sounds. In many cases, your first client can be the company you are about to leave. You simply continue to do the main parts of your current job but as a contractor instead of as an employee. The company saves huge fixed costs while you get the security of having that first client under your belt.

Build a Niche

You may remember the 1960s sitcom *Green Acres*. There was a character on the show named Mr. Haney, who would suddenly pop up whenever anyone needed *any* type of product or service. For instance, Oliver might mutter under his breath, "I sure wish I could get rid of these moles," and, out of nowhere, Mr. Haney would appear. While handing his business card, he would dramatically announce, "Eustace Haney, here. Expert Mole Assassin at your service." No matter what your need, Haney was there with his business card and his expertise.

Bill Cosby once said, "I don't know the secret to success; but I do know that the secret to failure is trying to please everybody." You need to narrow down your consulting practice into a special niche; you need to become the expert's expert. I have worked with an accounting firm that focuses on determining the depreciation schedule for each individual part of a new building. This niche is so specialized that all of this accounting firm's clients are other accounting firms. Success is related to focusing on a narrow something that you do differently from and presumably better than all others. You need an expertise.

A consulting business is a great way to make a living. This is the business where you get paid for your expertise while offering you the ability to enjoy the freedom and independence of doing your own thing. Combine that with a low cost of entry, and many, such as myself, find the consulting business as a near ideal form of self-employment.

Alone or with Partners?

Hewlett and Packard. Sears and Roebuck. Johnson and Johnson. While these company names are so very familiar to us, we sometimes forget that these folks were once just a couple of entrepreneurs with a dream. Statistically speaking, businesses started by partners do better than businesses started by individuals. Choosing the right business partner, however, can be quite a challenge. A good business partner shares your vision and brings expertise in the areas in which you are inexperienced. Most importantly, it's someone who you can get along with, both during crises as well as the good times.

As you begin your new business, you may need to decide whether it is best for you to go it alone or take on a partner or partners. Here is a truth about partnerships. Having a partner multiplies both the chance of success as well as the chance of failure in a business. The negatives are rather obvious. Personality clashes (different visions, different temperaments, and different personalities) can sink a business. Want to see a blatant example of this? Rent a Three Stooges flick where Larry, Curley, and Moe go into the piano-moving business.

What will be the working arrangement between partners? For instance, will the partners all be doing the same thing or will each partner cover a different area of expertise? Successful partnerships can be built either way.

For instance, partners doing the same thing work well for some types of companies, such as barber shops, plumber shops, and electrician shops. They can relieve each other on days off, assure customers don't have long waits, share expenses, and be able to purchase more modern and expensive equipment to share.

Multiple disciplines can also work well for partners. A firm consisting of lawyers or doctors could have each member concentrating on a particular area of medicine or law, and the firms thus become a collection of complimentary services. I worked with a now-successful restaurant chain with three partners. One handled daily operations; one dealt with marketing and personnel, and the third was a financial wizard. Individually, none of the partners had the expertise to cover the whole package. Together they had every aspect of the company's needs well-covered.

Selecting Good Partners

Look deeper than mere opportunity when choosing a partner. While compatible skills and the availability of finances seem to be critical, just as much attention must be paid to the personal aspects of the relationship. Here are some important areas that must be considered.

Are the Dreams Aligned? A potential business mate should bring something substantial to the table—like deep pockets, industry connections, or a skill you don't have. Just as important is for you and your partner to share the same strategic vision. There will be conflict if you dream of having a chain of stores to rival Home Depot, and your partner is happy running a small neighborhood hardware store.

Know Your Partner. Sure, complementary skills and a shared vision are a good starting point, but you should never underestimate the importance of actually liking your partner. My friend Tom tells of an otherwise logical venture that failed simply because of a personality clash. While he had great respect for his partner professionally, there was absolutely no personal rapport between them. "We lived in two different worlds," Tom explained. "While we agreed on just about everything around the office, we had little in common personally. We differed in faith, family, movies we liked—even our politics was polar opposite." Tom knew it was time to get out when he realized that he even dreaded going to lunch with his partner. Tom found a way to profitably and peacefully end the partnership and he jumped at it.

Do Your Due Diligence. Even if you get along fine initially, ask for financial statements and a resume that includes the names and phone numbers of past investment partners. I recommend that each of you take a personality test and compare the results. And, just as in marriage, date a lot.

Hang around each other. Is there a good rapport? Can you both discuss disagreements in a positive manner, or does one person dominate or try to "win" all the time? Engage in some of the other forms of business collaboration, such as jointly bidding on projects, subcontracting with another firm or principal, engaging in cross-marketing efforts, or making mutual referrals.

While you're engaged in these less-involved forms of collaborating, observe the behavior of the person you're working with, listen to their "war stories," and notice your own emotional reactions to the interactions you have. Discuss hypothetical situations. *What if one of us is unable to work for six months? A year? What if one of us gets divorced? What if an employee is stealing from us? What if one of us wants out early? How do we decide on a possible acquisition?*

Discuss Possible Exit Strategies. The best time to decide on an exit strategy is before you actually enter into a partnership. The sad fact is that most partnerships are temporary. If you wait until the divorce to discuss it, the ending will be decided by a jury of your peers. Outline exit strategies, such as a buy-sell agreement, as part of your partnership agreement.

Decide How to Handle Disagreement. You are kidding yourself if you think you will not have disagreements. What you decide when you disagree is far less important than how you disagree. I was in a very successful partnership in the late 1990s. Since it consisted of two highly opinionated and creative fellas, there was a high chance of disagreements. We recognized this on the front end and put a process into place. All major decisions required mutual agreement. If we stayed deadlocked, we would take the dispute to a third party (a mutual friend that we did a lot of business with) and go with his decision. A funny thing about this arrangement, we never had a dispute go to the arbiter. We always discussed the issue until we reached a good mutual decision. I think we were both so focused on the business that we didn't want an outsider to make the call.

BUYING A BUSINESS

Probably the hardest way to go into business is to start from scratch. You have to do everything for the first time, make some tough decisions, and take a lot of initial risks. There is a much easier way to have your own business—buy an existing one. You will get an operation that's proven to work, has a developed product, and has a staff in place. You will still have the opportunity to make changes and be creative. Like all options, buying an existing business has some definite pros and cons. Let's look at some of these.

YOUR PARTNER, YOUR SPOUSE

There are countless businesses in which a husband and wife successfully operate. There are also countless marriages and businesses dissolved due to spouses unable to work together. If you are thinking about going into business with your spouse, consider the challenges of a regular business partnership. Then multiply the challenges you face in marriage. How does the future appear to you now?

Frankly, the odds are poor. One expert plugs spousal businesses with only a 5 percent success rate. That's quite a risk for any partnership. When dealing with a normal partner, this may be a risk worth taking. After all, if the business fails, you're just losing a partner; however for spouses, folding the business may be the least of your losses.

You should make your own evaluation of the risks of a spousal business partnership, but let me make these suggestions to help both your domestic and business partnerships survive.

Don't do it by default. Go into business with your spouse only if the two of you have mutually planned it and the partnership would still make sense even if you were not married. Don't do it simply because you have no other options.

It's not personal; it's business. Spouses usually speak to each other more bluntly than business partners do. Roles can be confusing, especially if one spouse holds a position in the business generally considered lower than the other's role. Learn to take business discussions in their business contexts.

Forget the stereotypes. Recognize that each of you have a set of skills. Develop your organization based on this, not along traditional gender roles.

Separate work and home. Schedule regular weekends with zero business. Treat obvious family events as family events. Have a social life that includes friends that are not clients. Have actual dates with business talk forbidden. Don't handle family issues at the office . . . and never in front of clients or employees.

These proposed solutions may have enlightened you on the *complexity and dangers* of spousal partners. If this brief discussion scared you, maybe you should delay having a spousal business until the issues have been worked out.

I do not like ending a section on such a negative note, so let me offer you this possible cake-and-eat-it solution. Consider forming two complementary businesses, such as a flower shop and a nursery. You could become customers and suppliers to each other. That way you can see each other regularly, discuss common support, and cheerfully chat about industry trends, while avoiding the routine conflicts that come during the course of daily business.

The Good News

- The business idea, model, and products will be proven, and the well established.
- There will be an existing customer base.
- The business will have years of experience available to you, which reduces risk in making financial forecasts, introducing new products, or considering investments.
- When you buy a business, you buy the team. Those employees will have years of experience and knowledge that you don't.

The Other News

- Someone selling a business will have invested a great deal of their own money and time. They will want to generate a significant amount of money in return for losing the annual profits from the business. You may have to pay a premium price to get a solid business.
- Image and reputation are set. Or at least it will be difficult to change them. Even if those things are quite good, it may take some of the fun out of it for you.
- If the seller has focused more on selling the business rather than running it, it may be a little run down. You may have to invest more than the purchase price for the business to be hitting on all cylinders.
- You will be bound to all existing contracts, including employees, suppliers, and customers. Taking on staff someone else hired can be an interesting challenge, especially if the seller was very popular with employees. Winning them over may be a challenge.

Here is the most important piece of advice I can possibly give you—do your due diligence. Do not skimp on this. Enlist a skeptical accountant and shark-like attorney to help you investigate the books, the contracts, and every claim made about the business. Interview the key employees if possible. Talk with some of the clients or customers. Even if the seller is well known to you and considered a really great guide, remember that even the best people can be overly optimistic or just unaware of realities. Make sure you are going into your new venture with your eyes wide open.

Franchising a Business

Franchising might be your ticket for owning a successful business. The concept offers a unique set of pros and cons. If you are a security-sensitive entrepreneur, you will like the system in which the operations and marketing systems have already been worked out and proven to work; how-

---

SEEK PROFESSIONAL HELP

Betty always wanted to own her own business and was excited when she found the ideal one for her. It was a small shop selling books and crafts in a great location. The FOR SALE sign in the window lead her to immediately go inside and meet with the owner. He was a very nice man who asked for a small purchase price along with her assuming the rather large rent. Betty examined all the books. The unusually heavy sales easily covered the high rent as well as the monthly obligations.

Betty bought the business and immediately invested more cash into expanding the inventory, including adding an exclusive line of greeting cards. Despite the improvements, sales began to slip. By the end of the first year, Betty realized sales were off 38 percent from what the previous owner did the previous year. She was casually talking with her best salesperson about the sales issue when she told Betty something rather shocking. "Sales aren't down; they are actually up," she stated. "Frank had another business. He ran those sales through here. I thought you knew."

Betty had just given the books a cursory look and never secured the assistance of a forensic accountant. She lost $150,000—all of her savings—and closed up shop. Three years later, when I asked her why she didn't sue the previous owner for fraud, Betty softly replied, "I didn't know I could." Not only had she failed to employ an accountant, she had not consulted with an attorney. An attorney who would not only have told her the previous owner had committed both a civil and criminal act, but that she had a two-year statute of limitations for filing suit.

---

ever, one of the downsides of franchising is that you that you won't have as much control as you would in a business you started yourself.

Perhaps the biggest advantage of buying a franchise business is that it is generally a lot less risky than starting a new one. U.S. Department of Commerce studies show that over 90 percent of new businesses fail within three to five years. In comparison, over 92 percent of franchised businesses are still operating after five years. With a proven operating system already in place, franchises can generally offer you a much greater chance of establishing a successful business. (Note: When was the last time you saw a McDonald's go out of business?)

One critical part of any management system is solid training. A franchise system should have a proven training system as part of its program. Not only that, credible franchise organizations will provide ongoing training for you and your employees. Most important for you is the initial training you will be required to complete. You can enter most programs with no specific business knowledge about the company's operations and then learn, in a couple of months, all details you need to credibly function.

Providing ongoing support to franchisees is second nature to most franchise companies. This is because it is in their best interests for you to succeed; the better you do, the more money they make. Here are some further support systems you can expect:

- **Ongoing operational assistance.** You will have someone assigned as your franchise representative, who will be in regular contact with you. She will provide advice, news, and regular inspections to assist in the successful operation. (Kinda like a helpful boss/partner that thinks of you as the customer.)

- **Real Estate Assistance.** Not just manuals and advice, most franchises will become rather active in selection of real estate. In fact most will require their evaluation and approval of any new sites. This increases your chances of success as it brings the franchisor's experience and knowledge into this critical decision.

- **Construction Assistance.** Not only will they help you select and negotiate with contractors, franchisors have opening systems to help you smoothly and efficiently open your new facility. This includes equipment lists, prenegotiated supply prices, and stock lists so you open with the correct inventory. This saves you a lot of cash in the opening of your business.

- **Purchasing Power.** Most franchisors pass down the huge savings caused by the company's tremendous purchasing power. Again, these savings adds up.

- **Marketing Assistance.** Not only is a franchise organization big enough to employ the best ad agencies and have a heavy media presence, but the sheer numbers of franchisees make the brand a household name. You could never have that kind of clout as an individual owner.

Does this seem like paradise? In the spirit of bringing balance to the universe, let me point out that you must give up something to get all these benefits. The biggest thing you give up is control. Most of the things listed as "assistance" are actually required for franchise owners. You have no actual control over the concept or the product. While you are allowed to add to the list, your marketing campaigns are pretty well set by corporate. When you buy a franchise, you're not just buying the right to use the franchisor's name, you're buying its business plan as well. Some days you might feel like a just a poorly paid manager working 80-hour weeks. An entrepreneur without control is an oxymoron.

Franchisors make a lot of money, and this money all comes from you. The most obvious consideration is royalty income. They trade you their operating system and good name for a percentage of sales. While this is usually a reasonable trade, be aware that it often motivates the franchisor to come out with new products and big marketing campaigns designed to raise sales with little regard to profitability.

Also, franchisors charge a fee just for the right to become a franchisee. While much of this fee goes to cover their cost in assisting you to open facilities, there is also a cost of entry that's just for joining their family. This, in itself, could be hundreds of thousands of dollars.

THE ELEPHANT IN THE ROOM

You are probably thinking, "This has been an interesting discussion, Ken, but lets get real. Don't you realize the economy sucks?" Yes, I do. In fact, the bulk of this book was written at the peak of the worst economy since the 1930s. (I hope at least this is bad as it gets.) But crisis brings remarkable opportunities. I actually agree with Donald Trump who says that this is the best time in our lifetime to be an entrepreneur. How is that? Think about what an entrepreneur needs to start a business and to build that enterprise. Let's evaluate the list:

Bargains Are Everywhere. Bad economic times means that many people are suffering. Prices are tumbling in almost everything you need to start and run a business. Land and office space, equipment, and construction can all be had at cheap prices, sometimes even at desperation prices. (Do you need to purchase automobiles or pickup trucks? Jackpot!) Check the auctions and clearance centers for incredible bargains. Your new business will benefit because a low startup cost significantly lowers your risk as well as the monthly nut you must crack.

You Can Hire Some Great People and at a Bargain Rate. Even companies with bright blue chips are consolidating, merging, and becoming leaner. They are leaving in their wake an army of solid, well-qualified professionals who will work for a reasonable rate.

Downsizings Create Great Business Opportunities. Most downsizings involve transferring the needed services from employees to independent contractors. The work still needs to be done, creating myriad opportunities for entrepreneurs. Combine this need with the plethora of available talent and you can see why Trump calls this the greatest time ever for entrepreneurs.

Companies Are Looking to Change Suppliers. It is no secret that prices are falling. Other businesses want to take advantage of possible value and cost savings. Companies are seeking better deals from their suppliers. If you can offer a better deal or greater efficiency, customers will beat a path to your door.

Suppliers Are Offering Better Credit. Because traditional credit markets have virtually shut down, business-to-business credit sources are keeping money circulating out of necessity. That means great terms for your company's inventory—especially at startup.

You Can Find Some Great Deals When Buying an Existing Business. A lot of people currently in business are scared. They don't know how to trim costs or build sales and are eager to get out while they can. Plenty of businesses can not only be found at a low price but on incredible terms.

There Is a Lot Less Competition. "Conventional wisdom" is that this is a lousy time to start a business, so most conventional businesspeople are sitting this one out. Fewer people are in the market means there are more opportunities for you.

Most Businesses Do Poorly in a Down Economy. (Actually, I guess that's what makes it a down economy.) Let's face it, this is a lousy time to own an auto dealership, a residential real estate firm, or a construction company. These people are trapped in these businesses. But you are not. You get to pick your business with the full knowledge of what is viable and what is not. You don't have to dig yourself out of any holes. Obviously, pick from industries that offer grand opportunity.

✳✳✳

Making the leap into self-employment is a big decision in your life. Being a Boomer is a big advantage since you bring many experiences to the table. You are mature enough to be primarily guided by solid logic while still young enough to be influenced by some good healthy enthusiasm.

I hope you can combine these traits as well as a cousin of mine. He had spent his youth working in the back of his father's taxidermy shop. Later in life, after about 10 years off and on in college, he received his DVM (doctor of veterinary medicine) degree. That was when he opened up his first business; combining his veterinary clinic with his father's taxidermy shop. The business did just OK for a year and then he brought in a partner to handle finance and marketing. And it was with a single stroke of genius that the partner showed his value. Business exploded when my cousin introduced his new tagline:

Snellville Veterinary Clinic and Taxidermy Shoppe

Either Way You Get Your Dog Back

Maybe this chapter held little interest for you, or after reading it you are more terrified of risk than you were before. Whatever the cause of your lack of enthusiasm, follow your instincts. Self-employment is certainly not for everyone. In fact, it's not for most people. If your gut says no, it is most certainly right. It's just not for you. Focus your strategy on one described in the previous chapters.

MEET JIM CALVERT, CEO OF INVENTORY MANAGEMENT ANALYSIS, TORONTO, ONTARIO

Jim Calvert began his business carrying all the excitement that normally comes with the start of a major venture. But like most of us, it also came with something else—some good, healthy fears. "My biggest barrier of entry wasn't funding, or experience, or potential customers," he states. "It was the fear factor. Really a whole series of fears." His list included:

- fear of failure, what if it doesn't work?
- fear of the unknown; leaving a secure, comfortable place to go who-knows-where?
- fear of future regret; not wanting to ask "what if?" years from now.

For Jim, the timing was right for starting his own business. He was a sales manager and had had great success for several years. While the work was still satisfying, he knew he would soon need some greater challenges for his life. Jim had already begun outlining the business concept—which he had named Inventory Management Analysis (IMA)—when he learned that his company had been sold to a large, faceless conglomerate.

Time for a family meeting. He gathered his wife and two teenage daughters and discussed the situation in detail. They discussed the leap from security into an unknown future, the pros and cons of the venture, and his fear that he would forever regret his decision if he didn't try. His family gave him their support, which was the most important thing Jim needed for his decision. "At that point," Jim said, "I knew I had to do it."

Jim then had the opportunity to have his cake and eat it too. The day after he gave his notice, the owner of the acquiring company called him. It seems that Jim was one of the reasons they had purchased his company; they asked that he stay on, at least temporarily, and train the sales staff. Jim agreed and started IMA while still drawing a nice paycheck. IMA consisted of Jim, two employees, and no customers. Twenty years later, IMA is a successful international business that has become the fulfillment of everything he and his family could have hoped for.

Jim is eager to share what he has learned with future entrepreneurs. Here is some solid advice for those contemplating their own business:

- Believe in who you are, present with passion, see and feel what your audience is doing.
- Look at customers as partners as they are crucial to your success of failure.
- Your credibility always stays with you. Build a solid reputation and quality relationships; you can use that to network and build the business.

- It is important that you stay focused and specialized, become the best at your specific niche. If a customer wants something outside of that core, use your network to find someone to help them rather than straying from your expertise.

- Honestly evaluate and recognize your strengths and weaknesses. By knowing these you can make better decisions as to who to hire, how to retain customers, and how to delegate.

- Most important: Recognize that it's the people that determine your company's success. Treat employees like the golden asset they are.

Retirement? It seems to depend on the definition of the word. While Jim has made arrangements for the transfer of operations to others in every aspect except one, Jim will remain the face of the organization, presenting IMA's package of services to prospective clients around the world. "I can only retire if I find someone with the same drive and passion I have," he says. Based on that criterion, Jim Calvert should be around IMA for a long, long time.

Chapter 10

Dreams Never Retire

Boomers will redefine aging the way we have redefined so much of during our "tenure." In the past, we retired our so-called old folks because they weren't going to live much longer anyway. Besides, we had plenty of the next generation eager to take their place. Now, we Boomers may live much longer and healthier in our retirement years as they did in the career years. And for the first time in history, there are a lot more of us than there are of the next generation. We Boomers have the ability to redefine both "career" and "retirement" to mean whatever we want the words to mean. Besides, employers needing talent really don't have any alternative place to turn.

If any one word summarizes the Boomer generation, that word would have to be "change." And nowhere in our lives is that more apparent than when speaking about retirement. One reason for the difficulty in describing Boomer retirement is because with Boomers, we honestly don't know what that means. The definition has changed so much that it encompasses activities as varied as continuing to work full time, owning a new business, volunteering full-time, traveling the world—and all combinations thereof. In Boomers' future lives, it will be difficult to know when the working years end and retirement begins.

About 75 percent of Boomers intend to stay in the workforce even when they reach the age of traditional retirement. In the past, most workers considered retirement as the end. Boomers have changed that perception forever. Boomers perceive retirement as an exciting and *important* phase of our lives. Now that certainly does not mean we want to keep up the nine-to-five grind, but it does mean that we want a complete revolution to the whole concept of nine-to-five. Perhaps that time will now be used

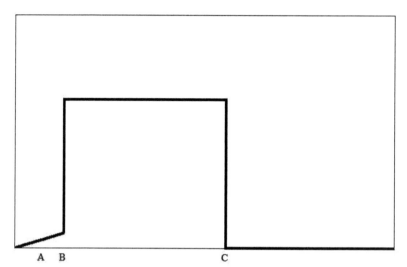

Figure 10.1 The Traditional Retirement Model

for volunteering or a second career, or for travel, or any of an unlimited variety of self-actualizing activities. (Lots more on that later.)

Let's look at two visual models. The first model represents the traditional view of retirement (Figure 10.1).

Explanation: In Figure 10.1, (A) the Boomer works part time in his teen years and during college. Work is purely a function on earning extra money and rarely career related. (B) The worker begins a career and usually works several decades until (C) one day (usually the 65th birthday), he retires. In that one day, the worker goes from total concentration on his career to doing nothing more than laying on the couch waiting to die. (Yes, a terrible exaggeration but let me make the point contrasting it with the Boomer model.)

Explanation: In the second model (Figure 10.2), points (A) and (B) are the same as in the traditional model, but at some point during the career, (C) the Boomer starts valuing his hobby, avocation, new business, second job, and so on, more than with his primary career. This new venture takes on more and more value, and the career takes on less value until one day the new venture has more worth (time, money, etc.) to the Boomer than does the primary career. It is at this point (D) that the Boomer is now considered retired. The Boomer continues this trend until one day, the venture receives his full attention and the so-called career gets none.

Now as I explained earlier, these graphs are gross simplifications. The trend line might be dramatically steeper or shallower, and the career line is rarely a straight horizontal. But I use them to make the point. With our

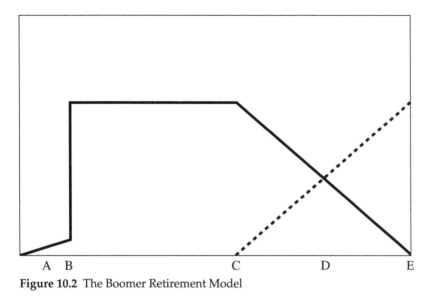

Figure 10.2 The Boomer Retirement Model

JOE COLETTA, MINNEAPOLIS, MINNESOTA

Joe is a young 60 and has been a salesman for four decades. He underwent a lung transplant about five years ago, giving him a new perspective on what he values in life. He is committed to this philosophy: "If there is something out there I want to do, then by golly I am going to do it."

Despite his many illnesses—*or perhaps because of them*—Joe cannot see himself ever retiring. He enjoys the interaction with his customers. He is proud of his products and humbly admits he is pretty darn good at selling them. Joe's interest in continued employment is not really making more money, it is making the best use of his talents. He has fine-tuned the ability to read a person's verbal and non-verbal cues and knows how to anticipate what their needs will be. Learning about a person's life and finding the small details are what makes Joe not only a good salesman but also a good friend to those he works with.

Joe has reached a level in his company that allows him to set his own hours. He normally starts his day at 4 A.M. by sending a few e-mails. He then makes a few calls while driving to the office, then meets with several customers and caps it off with lunch with one of those customers. He then heads home where he enjoys his family as well as some personal activities. For instance, Joe is a big fan of the blues. He regularly attends the Blues Fest in Duluth as well as similar events in the Twin Cities area. He also likes to collect oddities from movies such as his recently purchased Superman-style phone booth.

Using the traditional definition, Joe Coletta will never retire. But by the Boomer definition, he already has.

grandparents, retirement was an easily identifiable event; you could point to the specific date. The new Boomer retirement just doesn't work that way. It is a transition. It is more of a process than an event.

This transition is the most significant social trend we are currently seeing. The new Boomer model shows the competing visions for work that are already lining up to capture the hearts and minds, and the time, of Boomers who are not content to spend their next 30 years on the golf course or on their sofa. Boomers are searching for a calling in the second half of life; we are moving beyond midlife yet refusing to fade away. If the old dream of retirement was *freedom from work*, the Boomer dream is the *freedom to work*—in new ways, on new terms, with new meaning. While retirement used to signal the end of a productive life for workers, Boomers now see retirement as a transition point for beginning a new phase of our lives. For those approaching retirement, it is now a time to develop a strategy to work fewer hours, try a new career or business, learn new skills, further one's education, give back through volunteering, and enjoy life.

TRADITIONAL RETIREMENT ISSUES

Social Security

Let's discuss this obvious issue: Will Social Security be around when we retire? The answer is, quite simply, yes. As to what form it will take is the real question. As you know, Social Security was created as a well-funded Ponzi scheme. As devious as that sounds, it actually was a stable program, that is, until two aberrations occurred. The first problem that threw off the math was that Social Security grew from a small supplemental payment into a check that was supposed to fund a person's total monthly expenses. In the 1950s, for example, air conditioning combined with large Social Security checks to sponsor one of America's great migrations as senior citizens moved from the Northeast to sunny Florida. This migration started the new image of retirement in which when you turned 65 you could move to a nice resort and Uncle Sam would pick up the tab. Unfortunately, the benefits became too large to support the original math.

The second thing that caused the Ponzi scheme to fail was, well, us. While the Boomers have done a lot of things right, we have had one massive failure. We did a lousy job reproducing. The successive generation is 20 percent smaller. The New Deal planners never dreamed that the United States would have a generation less numerous than its parents', so again the formula collapsed.

And there is yet another reason that the formula has fallen. And that is that we, unfortunately, have been living much longer. When Social

Security was first conceived, the average American man lived to be 58. Now with all the medical advances, better diet, and a dramatic drop in smoking, the typical Boomer man will live to see his 75th birthday; women will make it well past 80. (An interesting perspective here. In our grandparents' time, old age was anything over 60. Today, we consider 60 as middle age.)

But there is cause for some optimism. The Social Security system is solvent until 2042, even if we do nothing. The youngest Boomers will be 78 years old in 2042, the oldest will be pretty much be dead. Sorry, I'm being flippant. But my point is that even if we do absolutely nothing, we're OK for a few more decades. And if we do "do something"—for instance a five-percent increase in Social Security taxes—the program will be solvent indefinitely.

And, while the older Boomers did a lousy job reproducing, the younger Boomers and GenX did a much better job. They have been good enough to reproduce like bunnies; in fact the newest generation, the Millennials, is experiencing what is being called the second Baby Boom. These Millennial munchkins start hitting the workforce with some significance (read paying Social Security taxes) in 2020, just in time to shore up our retirement.

And one further cause for optimism. Social Security is controlled by Congress. The only reason any member of Congress ever does anything is to get votes. And who controls the electorate for the next 20 years? Yep, we do. I think it is safe to predict that Congress will do what it needs to do to keep Boomer voters happy.

But even with this, don't expect to be able live on your government benefits. Even under the most optimistic scenario, the concept of Social Security will never go back to what it was in the 1950s. It will never again be adequate to fully support sipping pina coladas in Miami. Franklin Roosevelt's original vision of Social Security will have come full circle.

As It Is Today

Let's take a quick look at one aspect of Social Security as it stands now. We Boomers are turning 62 at the rate of 365 an hour and will continue to do so through 2026. Current rules allow people to begin drawing Social Security when they turn 62 at a benefit reduced by 25 percent of that paid at full retirement age. About half the people immediately take the reduced benefit and half wait for the full retirement age. It's important to note that the full retirement age is no longer 65. In order to reduce the total payout from the Social Security fund, that age was increased, starting with those born in 1943.

Year of Birth	Full Retirement Age
1943–54	66 years
1955	66 years and 2 months
1956	66 years and 4 months
1957	66 years and 6 months
1958	66 years and 8 months
1959	66 years and 10 months
1960 and later	67 years

"PAY NO ATTENTION TO THAT MAN BEHIND THE CURTAIN!"

This discussion on Social Security is not meant to be a reference to the program or a technical description of how to use it. I'm not trying to address any type of financial planning in this book. I am not competent to give financial advice. Don't you dare interpret anything I say in this book as financial advice. I warn you, if you do, your 401(k) will look like mine. Not a pretty sight. Rather I am trying to help you understand the intent of Social Security and how it will play into the retirement plans for the Boomer.

Your decision to take your benefits now or wait until later depends on two big factors: how long you expect to live and how good you are at managing your investments. You will only be paid 75 percent of your full benefits—for the rest of your life—if you opt to begin withdrawing at age 62. If you wait until eligible for full benefits, in my case age 66 plus two months, you will draw 100 percent for your full life. And for those really patient folks, you will receive 132 percent in you wait until age 70.

My analysis (and remember, I'm no expert) is that if you expect to be healthy and live to an old age, it would make sense to wait until full benefits or even later; however, if you see a hooded man in a black robe lurking in the near distance—or if you are good at investments—early withdrawal might work to your favor.

The Pension versus the 401(k)

Remember pensions? Some of you may still participate in one, especially if you work for a government entity. Pensions were an effective retirement funding tool for the worker. The employer put in a regular contribution (as did the worker), and a defined benefit (based on a formula derived from your income and years of service) was paid upon retirement and for the rest of your life. The pension solved a lot of problems. One was that it forced people to save for retirement. And second, payments continued for the rest of your life, so you didn't have to worry about outliving your income.

Unfortunately, most companies replaced pensions with self-directed 401(k)s. (They've got to come up with a new name for these things. It sounds like a sportscar or a cleaning formula.) As good Americans, we crave independence and the freedom to make our own decisions and the 401(k) seems to satisfy the needed requirements. We determine how much money to put in, we decide when to put it in, and we choose the financial vehicles to use. ("No sissy T-bills for me!" many of us said. "I want turbocharged high-growth stocks!") Unfortunately, many of us started late and contributed little, and the market (especially for turbochargers) tanked. Many of us who applauded the switch to 401(k)s are missing the old-fashioned pension something awful.

Do You Want a Pension Plan? Here's a Way

While I am not a financial expert, I am a nationally recognized expert on the subject of employee attrition. And let me give you some ammunition should you chose to lobby management for a return to a pension plan from the murky waters of the 401(k).

There has been an unfortunate consequence when a company shifts from pensions to 401(k)s. Employee turnover dramatically increases. Defined benefit plans gave employees a powerful reason to stay around and be loyal to their company. Self-directed instruments, which by definition are portable, actually encourage folks to pack their bags and see what's around the next bend.

Why should employers care? Switching to 401(k)s let them save a few bucks and that is a good thing, right? Here's why they should care—employee attrition costs the company between one to five years salary for the loss of each manager and about 6 to 12 months for each clerical employee. (Key sales representatives, senior managers, product development specialists, brand managers, and so forth can easily cost the company well over a million dollars when they leave.)

Instead of an efficient, 30-year professional (who stays in order to maximize his pension), the company has a succession of about a dozen employees who leave as soon as they get the skills they needed to grow their career. Or they take off as soon as they are bored. Or even when the competition offers them a $50 a month raise. Without a progressively growing pension plan, they have no incentive to stay!

BEING SELFISH IS THE SELFLESS THING TO DO

If you have children, you may be struggling with the question of where to put your savings—in a retirement fund or a vehicle for your children's college education? Our first urge is to take care of our children before ourselves, but CNN consumer guru Clark Howard urges the opposite. In fact, it may be in everyone's interest (including the kids) for you to focus on retirement savings first.

The children will be able to pay for college no matter what happens. There are lower-cost colleges, scholarships, and student loans available for them, but nobody will make a retirement loan for you. Sure, the kids might enter their careers carrying some low-interest debt, but at least they won't have the burden of worrying about and possibly supporting dear old Mom and Dad.

Get with your company management, the HR department, and the CFO and begin a dialog. Let them know you would prefer a return to a pension plan. Show them the real cost savings they would have in addition to improved efficiency and morale. Everybody wins.

First let's deal with the guilt we have been laying on ourselves. While many of us have done a good job saving for retirement with IRAs and 401(k)s, some of us haven't. Despite the many vehicles created to make saving easier, there are a lot of folks that have accumulated little or nothing. With retirement looming, this creates a scary situation and a lot of us Boomers are trembling and kicking ourselves.

Before we get into some solutions, let's address the self-flogging. The fact is that life happens. It's tough to stockpile cash to be used 40 years in the distant future when you have a young family, and you are trying to save for a house or simply have some sort of life while you try to get your career going. Early on in your career, retirement savings can hit pretty low on the priority list.

Others just never faced the reality that the day would ever actually come. For them, retirement planning was a lot like buying furniture at *Rooms To Go*. You know how they offer a deal where you can buy thousands of dollars worth of furniture and make no payments until 2013? I can't comprehend it ever actually getting to be 2013, besides, there's a good chance the rapture will occur well before then anyway. When you are 31 years old, it's hard to put away money you needed *right then* for some day in the future that you cannot comprehend will ever arrive. So, many Boomers didn't save.

Then again, those who were responsible did see that day coming, and they did something about it. They took advantage of all the retirement vehicles available. They used dollar cost averaging to build a sizable portfolio that was destined to take care of them in the proverbial golden years. And then they lost a huge chunk in the late nineties (dot.com fiasco), more in the shadow of 9/11, and then again in the fall of 2008. All that work and all that planning and all that discipline, and they are not a whole lot better off than those grasshoppers who never quite got around to saving at all.

No matter what your savings situation, those of you who are retiring in the next few years face some very real problems. Most of us will address the realities by continuing to work past 65, either on a full-time or part-time basis. There are a couple of other options to look at. Please note that when I say "look at" I mean exactly that. Remember I am in no way qualified to advise you on any financial matter. (Legions laugh uproariously at the mere suggestion.) If you promise not to take any of this as financial advice, let me toss out a few directions you may want to *look at*.

Immediate Annuities

Read that idea again. I said *immediate* annuities, not *deferred* annuities. Deferred annuities have been pretty well discredited by most financial advisors, but an option for you to consider in order to stretch your retirement savings might be immediate annuities. As the name suggests, you give the insurance company a big chunk of money today, and your payments begin immediately and continue for the rest of your life. "Why should I do that," you are thinking, "when I could just put the money in the bank and withdraw a bit every month myself?" Yes, you could do that and you would save all sorts of management fees and broker commissions; however you need to ask yourself, "How much can I withdraw each month?" These days life expectancy for someone age 65 is about 18 more years. Should you base your withdrawals on that statistic? Wait! You must also consider that while the average lifespan gives you 18 more years, there is also a good possibility you will live longer than that—as much as 40 more years! Planning for that possibility really shrinks the amount of cash you can safely withdraw each month.

So there is the dilemma. Do you base your withdrawals on the average lifespan and risk running out of money, or do you base it on the maximum lifespan and reduce your lifestyle dramatically? The insurance company doesn't have to ask that question. They can base their cash flow on the *average* itself—by definition half of their clients will die earlier than the average and half will live longer. So, the math works out for them just fine. But you are protected by having a set income each month that never expires (until you do.)

Use Your House

About 80 percent of us Boomers own our homes, and we have substantial equity in them. That cash, while showing up on our personal balance sheets, doesn't do squat in improving our cash flow. Consider these three strategies for having your house take care of you in retirement.

Sell It. This is a rather obvious solution, but one that could go a long way in funding your retirement without a reduction in your standard of living. How's that? While we tend to base our future needs on the ones we have today, our current needs and future needs are rarely the same, are they? For instance, today we might need a house with five bedrooms (for the three teenagers), three baths, and three or four cars. We are either saving for or putting out a lot of money for college, as well as forking over thousands to keep the little fellers clothed, fed, and groomed with the occasional haircut. In addition, the cost of gasoline for the 40-mile commutes adds up as well as payment for parking spaces once you get there.

Now I could go on and on describing these costs but you get the idea; the costs will be dramatically reduced once the munchkins are out on their own (which we all fervently hope is well before our retirement.) But more importantly, you just don't need as big of a house when the kids move out. In fact, because of the drastic reduction in expenses, you could maintain your same standard of living in a much smaller house (on the beach or by a lake?).

Selling the house does involve real estate fees and such, but if you take that money and seriously downsize your living quarters, you have some serious cash to redistribute to retirement expenses.

Take Out a Home Equity Line of Credit. Only rarely would this make a whole lot of sense, but I'll go ahead and remind you of the possibility. In order to take out such a loan, you have to prove to the bank that you have an ongoing stream of income that can be used to pay off the loan. And if you have one of those, why are you taking out a loan?

Where this strategy might work is if you are continuing to work part time and want to take care of some initial expenses that may come with the act of retirement. Usually we have a need for larger withdrawals in the early days of retirement than later, so in this rare case you might look to this option.

Get a Reverse Mortgage. This is one of those plans, like annuities, that work well because of the fact that someday you will die. The professionalism of the reverse mortgage industry has improved dramatically in the last 10 years. Reverse mortgages work somewhat like an immediate annuity only instead of you putting up an initial cash payment you transfer a percentage of your home's equity. Monthly payments are made until your death, at which time your home is sold and the investor is paid back an amount based upon what was negotiated when the contract was signed.

Note that the base investment is not the full value of your house. Actually, far from it. Current base lending is in the range of 30 percent of the equity. Also note the agreed-upon payments continue until your death, no matter how many years that may be. Like the instant annuity, the reverse mortgage amount is calculated from actuarial tables, so while it might be a bonanza for you, your long life is paid for by the guy who was hit by a beer truck right after he signed the papers.

As good as it looks initially, enter into this arrangement with care. What if the neighborhood deteriorates and the house value falls? What if the price of housing in general drops? And what if your kids move across the country and you want to move with them? Solving these problems is complex and costly; however, the reverse mortgage might be a good supplement to shortages in your retirement account.

Move

There are two possible courses of action whenever there is a shortage of money on the bottom line. One, you can increase revenue, or two, you can reduce expenses. Once you reach retirement age you might find it far easier to cut expenses than increase income. Perhaps the easiest way to reduce expenses is to move away from high-cost areas into those with a much lower cost of living.

We used to think that there was a good reason some places were expensive to live in, that they are more desirable places to live. While that is still certainly true for many great spots such as Hawaii, Southern California, Boston, and Chicago, it is not always so. In fact, there are many places having excellent standards of living at amazingly low costs.

It all depends on how *you* define a good standard of living. Large metropolises and the California coast are going to cost you a lot. But if you hate traffic and enjoy mountain views and lots of entertainment along with a very low cost of housing, look at Branson, Missouri. Warm weather most of the year with low costs? Look into southern Mississippi and Alabama. A large city with all the cultural and sports events at your doorstep? Take advantage of other people's economic disasters and move to cities like Detroit. Home prices have bottomed out while the positive parts of the city's infrastructure remain.

So much depends on what you consider to be desirable. Rate the things you want in a place to spend your retirement and then search for a place that excels in those particular features. Why pay for assets you don't need? For instance, if the kids are out of school, why pay the high property taxes you will find in areas with excellent schools? If you hate humidity and don't particularly care for the ocean, why pay the high costs of living in Miami? Move inland. While you may still have a lot of humidity, at least you're not paying for it. Have you been required to live in Manhattan for your job but yearn for the beach? Now is the time to score a bonanza in both quality of life and cost of living by moving to the Gulf Coast.

None of those cities ring your bell? How about these:

Fayetteville, AR	Ocala, FL	Daytona Beach, FL
Sarasota, FL	Ashland, OR	Oxford MS
Asheville, NC	Fairhope AL	Fredricksburg, TX
Portsmouth, NH	Chattanooga, TN	Spokane, WA
Charleston, SC	San Antonio, TX	Dahlonega, GA
Lincoln, NB	Eagle River, WI	Hamilton, MT
Mobile, AL	Savannah, GA	Bellingham, WA

These are just a few of the many excellent cities that offer a great standard of living at a surprisingly reasonable cost. The most extreme adjustment in cost of living in the United States is for those folks relocating to Dothan, Alabama, from San Francisco. They will find their expenses cut in half while maintaining the same lifestyle (assuming you *can have* the same lifestyle in Dothan).

Look, you probably live where you do now because either you grew up there or your last company transferred you there. If you don't have firm ties to where you are now, consider moving somewhere that offers all the features you really want at a much lower cost. A great source for doing this exploring is Rand McNally's *Places Rated Almanac*. It rates all 300+ metro areas in the United States and Canada for about a dozen different categories, including the cost of housing. The enclosed CD lets you decide how much weight to put on each category, and it will then print out a long list of cities ranked by your standards. (My wife and I used this method when I broke away from the corporate life and I could live anywhere in the country as long as there was telephone service. We fed our preferences into the program and it spit out a list of all the metro area ranked first to worst. The top four results for us were Honolulu, Knoxville, Boston, and Atlanta.)

Jerry Seinfeld once explained, "My dad just retired and my parents moved to Florida. They didn't really want to, but I think it's the law." Of course it's not, but many people do move to Florida after they retire—or to North Carolina, or Tennessee, or Arkansas, or to Montana, or to hundreds of other places. Many are seeking a better life at a lower cost. Retirement is a good time to reevaluate many aspects of your life and deciding where to live is a good way to start that evaluation.

WHERE DID THEY GET *THAT* NUMBER?

The traditional retirement age for the last hundred years has been age 65. Where did that number come from anyway? There is really nothing magical about it. In fact for much of the 20th century the average person was just lucky to live to be 65. Social Security began using that age as a benchmark in the 1930s, but they were just following the already established tradition. So, if not from Uncle Sam, where did it come from?

Like most rules and procedures about pensions, the precedents were established by the railroads. Somehow in its design of pension plans, the railroad industry decided that base retirement age was to be 65. While the reason for selecting this milepost has never been recorded, you might pick up a good clue if you understand the ruthless management style of the late 1800s. Since few people lived past 60, the railroads saved a fortune by rarely having to pay out much pension money. Thus, this firm impression we have is really not much more than our acquiescence to the schemes of a handful of robber barons.

BOOMER RETIREMENT

An LA lawyer becomes a chef in Sheffield, AL. A mechanic turns into a minister. A symphonic conductor becomes sympathetic counselor. A factory worker (who is paid by the piece) joins the Peace Corps. Longer life spans, concerns about outliving retirement savings, a desire to stay productive, and a craving for self actualization are convincing many Boomers in their fifties and sixties to make a radical career change. In fact, as many as 8 million Boomers have already launched "encore careers," positions that combine income with personal meaning and social impact. Of those workers surveyed who are not already in second careers, half are interested in them.

Boomers will work into traditional retirement years for several reasons. Some will start an "encore career" purely for the money—a supplement to their Social Security for instance. Others will do it because the thought of playing bridge and lying on the couch is abhorrent. They'll be looking for a reason to get out of the bed in the morning. For others, it's an added insurance policy against dwindling retirement accounts.

While many of these *recareerings* involve following a dream, you don't want to be completely consumed with the romance of the quest. If you watch a lot of movies, you can get seduced into thinking that all that you need to do is follow the rainbow and the details magically fall into place. It rarely works quite that way. Unless your name is Bob Newhart you just don't open an inn in Vermont and enjoy immediate success. We covered a good bit of this concept in chapter 9, but let's take a moment and look at these additional tips for preparing for your recareering.

Start Planning Early

Recareering is not something that you jump into at the last minute. There is too much to plan, to learn, and to explore to even consider doing anything with good solid preparation. The most important step in preparation is deciding what it is you want to be doing. Start by appraising two things: your abilities and your interests. Knowing your skills should come easily, simply inventory the many things (not just at work) that you have been doing for the last 20 or 30 years. Collect even those skills that have been a minor part of your life. Just because you haven't used them a great deal doesn't mean they are not marketable skills. And, as we learned in chapter 4, you don't have to be paid for something in order for it to be an accomplishment or skill. Many marketable skills can be polished in volunteering or as a hobby. Realize that all of your skills—regardless of their origin—can be transferred to your next career. Much of what you already know is transferable to your next undertaking.

The other half to be considered is figuring out what your dreams are. Now this shouldn't be too hard. If they are your dreams, you have probably been daydreaming about them for quite some time. But maybe it isn't that easy. Perhaps your dream has been a bit vague, such as simply wanting to be in business for yourself or wanting to help others. For those you have to do more digging and exploring; however, that exploration can be a great "hobby" for you. Exploring options can be fun, especially if you start doing it a few years before you plan to make the leap, so as I said before: *start planning early.*

There Is Always Room at the Top

You will have the easiest time finding your spot if you investigate jobs in the fields that are experiencing high growth. As previously mentioned, there is a strong need for workers in education, health care, and consulting, while real estate and most retail are having serious slumps. (A great tool for finding useful details about specific jobs can be found in the Department of Labor's *Occupational Outlook Handbook.* Visit the DOL Web site for ordering information.)

Now let me argue with that bit of advice for a moment. Actually the easiest spot for finding a job is in whatever field gets you the most excited. Your next job should be located at the intersection of your skills and your passion, regardless of the current job outlook. There are two reasons for me saying this. First, the job outlook is pretty much cyclical. While the real estate and construction industries may be depressed today, the outlook may be the absolute opposite two years from now. Enter into your "post-retirement" career with the same mindset you have always had; intend on staying in the career for the long haul.

But there is a more important reason to always go with your passion, and that is there is always room at the top. Realize that 10 percent unemployment is the same as 90 percent employment. I don't want to be flippant with such a serious matter, but you know that no matter what industry you choose, you will almost certainly land in the top 90th percentile! But beyond that, if there is a career field in which you have passion and skill, *you will fit in to the very top group of people in that industry.* Do not be frightened by people telling you that "engineering is overcrowded" or "this town already has too many restaurants" or "new home sales are only half of what it was a year ago". These things change every time a butterfly flaps its wings in China. And until that flapping occurs, remember that you will be at the top of the profession anyway. (One of the great things about discussing both sides of an issue is that when I look back I can always find a quote that proves I was right.)

Work Your Network

Yes, there is that word again. Networking is the cornerstone to building job referrals, business partners, personal assistance, and in placing yourself in a great recareered situation. In this case, form a weekly lunch or coffee group inviting all those who have gone through this situation or who, like you, are considering doing so. You can learn from the experiences of those that have made the move and swap ideas with those still cogitating. Soak up as much information as you can before making this decision. Talk with people who work in the potential industry. Sign up for an internship. Volunteer at a non-profit. Moonlight with a company in the industry. Remember that you do not have to work in the exact job to learn a great deal. Just being in the same industry allows you to evaluate the culture and routine that envelops the job.

Learn

If you are entering a completely new field, you probably need to acquire more training or education. It's a good idea to get that training while still on your old job so that you can enter the new job already fully prepared. Chances are you'll need to learn new skills and maybe even earn a degree in a new field. The same applies for the many positions that require licensing by the state or federal government. For instance, many police detectives become private detectives in their second life. Private investigators require licensing in most states, and it is far easier to get credentials while still employed by the police.

Professional programs, universities, and community colleges offer evening and weekend classes, which are relatively easy to fit into a nine-to-five schedule. All this can be quite expensive; don't let the cost of tuition scare you off. There's no age limit for getting a student loan. Also, take advantage of tax breaks. Depending on your income, you might qualify for the lifetime learning credit, worth up to $2,000 each year. If you make too much to qualify, you still might be able to claim a deduction associated with tuition and fees, up to $4,000.

One last note: earlier we discussed the need—and in some cases desperation—some industries are experiencing as we Boomers retire. Since the next generation is not as large as ours, a lot of jobs will go begging. These unfilled jobs are excellent opportunities for you, and many jobs come with a very special bonus—free on-the-job training. Keep your eye open for these opportunities as you explore your options.

Look at Your Checkbook

Your salary in your new career, at least at the beginning, will probably be less that what you are used to. As we discussed earlier, this can often be offset by a reduction in living expenses. Regardless of whether you plan to reduce your living expenses, let me recommend that you try living on the smaller amount before actually leaving the higher paid one. This practice will allow you to enter your new career with excitement rather than the

---

MEDICAL CONCERNS

You must investigate securing adequate health coverage should you choose to retire before your eligibility for Medicare (age 65). Individual policies often are prohibitively expensive—if they're available at all. Because we're often considered high risk, 20 to 40 percent of early retirees applying for individual insurance are either denied coverage or charged higher premiums.

Some companies offer health-care benefits to part-time employees, making them popular with older workers. Starbucks offers health-care benefits to employees who work at least 20 hours a week. Today only four percent of their workers are fifty or older, but that number has increased 50 percent over the past five years.

Although the trend is promising, very few companies match Starbucks's policy. In fact, just a fourth of companies that offer benefits for their full-time workers also offer them for part-timers. This issue makes it tough for those looking to retire before traditional retirement age. Study it carefully before committing to early retirement.

fear of having to constantly looking over your shoulder. Also, remember that if you are already receiving Social Security benefits, your new income may reduce those benefits.

WORKING AFTER RETIREMENT

Once a year I get a letter from the Social Security Administration projecting what my benefits will be once I reach retirement age. It's an interesting document, but probably just an intellectual exercise. Not because I expect the system to fail, but because I really never expect to stop working.

There is nothing particularly unusual about my attitude. A Merrill Lynch study estimates that 7 out of 10 adults plan to work to some degree after the age of 65. Half of those people plan to never stop working completely. Here are some more telling numbers from the U.S. Bureau of Labor Statistics. They project the number of employed Americans between the ages of 50 and 64 will actually increase by 51 percent between 2002 and 2012. Furthermore, those aged 65 to 74 will increase by 41 percent! How should we interpret this? It seems to me that the numbers are saying that a huge number of people over 50 are simply not going to retire. Or if they do, they won't be gone long. They'll be back working at least part-time soon afterwards.

While some Boomers will continue to work because they don't have a choice, most will do so out of choice. We're not ready to play just yet. We want to work.

And that is where we are fortunate. If you will remember, the older Boomers did a lousy job of reproducing. Because of this, the country is looking at a severe labor shortage *at all levels* as the Boomers reach retirement age. Therefore, rather than finding ways to usher workers out with a gold watch, companies are now trying to come up with strategies to entice older workers to stay.

Why Work? It's the Patriotic Thing to Do

There are a lot of reasons to continue to work instead of retiring. Money, a need to be active, and a search for self-actualization are some of the big reasons, but there is one more for you to consider. It's your patriotic duty. Your country needs you.

A study from the American Society of Training and Development shows that 79 million Baby Boomers will leave the workforce, but only 46 million workers will be available to replace them. To put a more immediate face to this phenomenon, the Bureau of Labor Statistics projects that by

2012 there will be 10 million more jobs than people. (I know—here in 2010 this doesn't seem possible.) This suggests a drop in production as well as productivity, impacts that the United States does not need to add to any current economic woes. Factored into that number is a serious shortage of highly skilled workers, experienced managers, executives, and professionals. These are shoes not easily stepped in to, suggesting it would be better to have current workers remain on the job rather than elevating subordinates.

Boomers welcome the news that we are about to be highly valued. While some companies are slow to realize this economic prediction, they are increasingly identifying the shift in workers' relative age (50 is the new 40) and are adjusting their hiring strategies. At the same time, faced with the recent tight economy and retirement portfolio declines, many Boomers are recognizing reality and postponing retirement. After all, it's the patriotic thing to do.

Your Value to Potential Employers

An important part of my business is in consulting with companies on building their teams and retaining their workers. I focus a great deal on the retention of older workers and how to lure great people out of retirement and into their workforce. Understand that I do not do this because of my dedication to Boomer employment. I am not using my consulting assignments to look after your rights and opportunities. I am giving companies that advice because hiring and retaining older workers is smart business for the companies.

For many Boomers nearing retirement, finding yourself back on the job market is difficult, scary, and frustrating. But know the new reality: your decades of experience are valuable and companies need it. Almost a third of companies surveyed are concerned about their loss of intellectual capital with retiring Boomers. Twenty percent indicate they are likely to rehire retirees from other companies. And that number will significantly increase once companies recognize the value of hiring retired workers. What are some of these important assets you bring to the table? For your self-confidence, as well as to help you realize the very real value you offer in the marketplace, let me touch upon some of the things you have to sell beyond "just" your particular set of skills. Here are some of the things I explain to the companies when I sell them the concept of hiring/holding on to older workers.

Retired Professionals Bring Clients with Them. If you are an accountant, doctor, engineer, attorney, or a member of any profession that collects clients as part of your work duties, realize that these former clients are a rich asset. There is a good chance that you can reestablish your relationships with former clients and bring them over to your new company or firm. This fact alone can more than justify a company hiring you.

Former Sales Executives Bring Their Customer List with Them. Just like the professionals, those with sales experience spent their whole career cultivating relationships with customers. Any competitor of you former company would leap at the opportunity to have your foot in the door. What is the value of just one good ongoing customer? Multiply that by the number of customers loyal to you and you'll have a pretty good idea of your value to the potential employer.

Older Workers Bring Their Experience with Them. Especially because of the general labor shortage, employers will have to spend a lot of money for training. Hiring an experienced worker saves most of that money. But the word "experience" means far more than basic skill training. An experienced worker understands the subtleties of the job, understands how to deal with people, and understands the solutions to all those walls he walked into on the other guy's dime. An experienced worker knows not just what needs to be done but why it needs to be done, as well as how it fits into the long-term goals of the company. But not only that, this experience is what makes an older worker such a great mentor to the other workers. An older worker enriches your whole workforce.

The Older Worker Can Relate to Older Customers and Clients. Not only are Boomer workers getting older, but so are Boomer customers. And since those Boomers make up the most numerous and wealthiest segment of the population, they will be the most important part of your customer base. For most products and services, customers prefer to deal with people they can relate to. Older customers will have a strong preference for Boomer employees.

And This May Surprise You. One reason some employers give for preferring younger workers is that of health. They say they just don't want to put up with a bunch of sickly old geezers calling in sick all the time. Well, guess what? Workers over 60 call in sick far less often than the Christophers and Jennifers of this world. I doubt that is because of their general health; more likely it is a function of the Boomers' work ethic.

NO SUCH THING

Are you a member of the American Association of Retired Persons? Sorry, this was a trick question. Actually, there is no longer any such organization. "We no longer call ourselves the American Association of Retired Persons because the word *retired* is a misnomer," says Bill Brown, Georgia spokesman for AARP. Between 40 percent and 45 percent of its membership is working.

ALTERNATE RETIREMENT FORMATS

As we discussed earlier, the traditional retirement—like the one your father took—had one form. You worked like a frenzied otter until your 65th birthday, you were handed a gold watch, and then you headed to the golf course. After a couple of hundred rounds you relaxed in your easy chair until you died. The Boomer retirement, on the other hand, takes on many forms and variations.

Working Part-time

There are three ways to arrange part-time situations. One is, of course, working half-days Monday through Friday, or full days three days a week (or any variation in between.) This is a good situation for professionals, such as attorneys and doctors, who can cut back on total hours but still give each client their full attention.

Another popular way is *job-sharing*, where you are matched with another worker and the two of you split the same position. A big benefit of job sharing is that during busy seasons both of you can go full-time, thus expanding the workforce when most needed. This is quite successful in retail—where you both go full-time during the holiday season as well as in restaurants, where you could overlap on Saturday nights. It is also a good strategy in the office environment, such as administrative assistants, receptionists, and other positions that have no direct reports.

Seasonal part-time work is another successful strategy. The employer can have your services during busy times and you take off all other times. Again, this is a groovy strategy for retail as well as some professions, such as tax accounting.

Phased Retirements

Phased retirement is the gradual tapering off of working hours and responsibilities, culminating in a final break from the company. This retirement method allows employers to fill urgent needs while transitioning to new leaders. For instance, General Electric has a program allowing retired employees to work up to 1,000 hours each year. IBM uses a phased retirement program in order to maintain a pool of retirees who mentor and teach the younger workers.

The Boomerang Year

Another option being considered by many employers is the Boomerang year. This is a form of the phased retirement in which you would take off a year or two before rejoining the company part-time. Several substantial companies have embraced the concept such as Polaroid, Monsanto, and Traveler's Group. This allows the company to benefit from your years of knowledge, while you get to take a long "vacation" before returning to work part-time.

From W-2 to 1099

This is an organized program assisting retirees in starting their own businesses. The company contracts your new business to perform some of the work you used to do when you were on their payroll. This benefits the company by their knowing that you understand their quality standards as well as the procedures and policies, as well as giving them the opportunity to influence you in your selection of other clients. (They don't want the knowledge they have given you to wind up benefiting a competitor.) Your benefit is obvious; you can set up your own operation and immediately land your first big client.

Enlist your current company as you plan your retirement. As shown above, there are so many ways they can benefit while helping you get your retirement off to a great start.

THE SELF-ACTUALIZED RETIREMENT

True story. Margaret Taft was asked to introduce herself on her first day of elementary school. She stood beside her desk and announced, "Hello, my name is Margaret Bowers Taft. My great grandfather was president of the United States. My grandfather was a United States senator. My daddy is ambassador to Ireland." Then she took a deep breath, held her shoulders back and proudly added, "And *I* am a Brownie."

As Maslow explained to us, the highest form of human existence is in our self-actualization. What is this? It is the point where all of our other needs are satisfied (food, safety, companionship, etc.), and we now have the time and ability to do those things that make us whole as a person. Volunteering. Helping. Learning. Expressing. Those things that tend to make our minds richer and our society better. Some of us, like Margaret Taft, are fortunate enough to be able to self-actualize at a young age. Other of us must wait until retirement to find the opportunity.

Ours is the first generation where the majority of its members will be able to embrace self-actualization as the main theme of our retirement years. In fact, many members will be working much harder at their self-actualizing activities than they did in their career jobs before.

Dreams Never Die

So what is the best use of your retirement? Perhaps it is your opportunity to finally grab that star you've spent so many years reaching for. Your dream doesn't have to be complex or Nobel Prize worthy. It might just be something simple that has been lightly tugging at you for a few decades. Or the passion might be a newly charged activity that you recently learned about. No matter. Just realize that this is your chance to live that dream. Be like the folks listed below, a virtual alphabet soup of ambitions felt and dreams realized.

- Albert is taking early retirement at 60 and will fulfill a childhood dream by becoming a police officer.
- Betty will go to school full-time and get her bachelors degree in art history. But first she will get her GED.
- Charlie will travel the world, often with his grandchildren. After that? More travel.
- Dan plans a relaxing retirement with a lot of golf and old movies; however, to bring in some extra cash and get free admissions, he's going to sell concessions in the stands at Royals and Chiefs games.
- Evelyn will retire, "Kind of." She will keep her same job in retail sales, but go to a part-time status.
- Frank has the exact same birthday as his boss. And on their 65th birthdays, Frank will watch his boss retire and then sign the papers to buy his business.
- Geraldine plans to take it easy and do a lot of gardening, specializing in breeding prize-winning roses.
- Henry has no plans to ever retire, but he will expand his role as head of the mentorship program where he works.
- Ilene will retire next year, at age 62. She is looking forward to working harder than ever volunteering at her church. She also plans on going on a new mission trip every six months.
- Jerry retired as a police officer four years ago when he turned 50. He now owns a successful detective agency, where he wears a fedora, "just like the detectives did in the old film noirs."
- Kent is spending his retirement active in local politics. He is eager to fulfill a lifetime ambition and run for the county commission next year.
- Lester became a minister after taking early retirement from a major computer company five years ago.
- Martha will keep working until her husband retires in two years. They then plan to take a lot of long walks and see a lot of old movies. (They own a collection of every Academy Award winner for Best Picture.)

- Nathaniel will do "nothing special" except take advantage of his state's program allowing those 60+ to audit courses at any state college for free. Nathaniel figures he might as well learn Spanish and French.

- Oliver and Pam will move to their lake house and do a "lot of fishin'." And while Oliver cleans the fish and piddles in the garage, Pam intends to write that novel she's been thinking about for 20 years.

- Quentin is hanging up his medical practice and joining the Peace Corps.

- Robert is going to expand his side business of flipping houses into a full-time occupation. He figures he will work harder and make more money than he ever has.

- Sue spent her Saturdays volunteering at the soup kitchen for the last nine years, but now that she is retired she will be working there five days a week.

- Tom just bought a boat. 'Nuff said.

- Ursula got a paying position with a charity she had been active in for many years. "Now I feel like I am doing something meaningful with my life, still volunteering, but actually getting paid for it." She adds that she'll leave this job "only when they carry me out on my deathbed." Ursula says she has no idea when work ended and her retirement began.

- Victor has obtained his teacher's certifications and will teach third grade beginning next fall.

- William plans on working as a VP in a branch bank, then build furniture in his garage the rest of his life. "I might sell some, give some away. Doesn't really mater as long as folks use it and enjoy it."

- "Xena" (not her real name) is a huge fan of science fiction. She plans to attend every Star Trek and other sci-fi conventions she can find anywhere in the United States.

- Yvonne will "read everything ever written by James Michener. And then I'll start on John Steinbeck."

- Zach declares that once he is released on parole, he will draw Social Security and stay out of trouble. And "get me a 50-inch widescreen TV with cable."

We all have our dreams. The smart ones find a way to live those dreams. I'm thinking you are one of the smart ones.

Coda

NO BUGLES, NO TRUMPETS

Few will have the greatness to bend history itself, but each one of us can work to change a small portion of events, and in the total of all these acts will be written the history of this generation.

—Bobby Kennedy

I was born in 1955, smack dab in the middle of the Baby Boom. So were Bill Gates, Disneyland, McDonald's, and the civil rights movement, all of which have become metaphors of the Boomer generation. McDonald's reflects America's lifestyle and Disneyland, its fantasies. Bill Gates? His influence represents where the Boomers have reshaped industry, the way the world works, and how it communicates.

The civil rights movement was also born in 1955 with a courageous woman refusing to give up her seat to a white man on a public bus. Growing up in the South in the 1960s I can remember seeing whites-only water fountains, separate restrooms, segregated schools, and public swimming pools refusing entry to "the colored." And I recall my feelings upon hearing Walter Cronkite announce the assassination of Martin Luther King, Jr. in my hometown. Yet just 40 years after that horrible event, the civil rights movement could claim victory with the election of a black man to the presidency. Within half a lifetime—not even a blink in the span of history—blacks have seen themselves going from being regarded lower than livestock to holding the most powerful position on earth. Were Boomers responsible for the civil rights movement? Not completely of course, but we can claim credit for the fulfillment. The movement was in itself a metaphor for the incredible progress in social action occurring on our watch, including women's rights and questioning government authority.

Never in the history of mankind has there been so much social change as during our watch. Women? A caveman would club his future wife over her head instead of proposing. Fifty thousand years later, Johnny Carson was making women's lib jokes and mocking the very idea of women being equal to men. As the concept of female equality began picking up steam, even the most so-called liberal among us would never have considered a woman as a construction worker, police officer, firefighter, or boss of men. But within 20 years—a blink anthropologically—women are considered the full equal of any man. It's fair to say this occurred primarily because of the Boomer generation.

As a student of history and a closet anthropologist, I tend to agree with most that the greatest generation in American history was, well, the Greatest Generation.

But the possible reason for this is that they *faced* the greatest problems this country has ever seen. They handled them brilliantly, for sure, and they showed remarkable character while doing so. But we must recognize that they sure did leave a lot of undone business to our generation. And we should also recognize that we have made a lot of real progress during our still-unfinished term.

Because of the drop off in numbers (79 million versus 66 million), combined with our longer lifespans, Boomers will continue to be the politically, socially, and financially dominant generation for about 25 more years. During that time we'll still control government and the bulk of the nation's wealth. So today we are far from being a past-tense group of people. Just like our parents, we can be proud of our accomplishments while realizing we have left a lot of work behind for the next generation. But unlike our parents, we still have a few decades to complete our legacy.

I do wonder what that legacy will be.

Index

ABOUT THE AUTHOR

KEN TANNER is an Atlanta-based human resources consultant specializing in employee retention and career development. This is Ken's fifth book; previous titles include *Never Order Barbecue in Maine* and *The Entrepreneur's Guide to Hiring and Building the Team*.

PREVIOUS BOOKS BY KEN TANNER

The Entrepreneur's Guide to Hiring and Building the Team, 2008, Praeger

Never Order Barbecue in Maine: Proven Career Strategies from People Who've Been There, Done That, 2006, Thomas Nelson Publishers (Korean edition, 2007, Seoul Shinmun Publishers)

Retaining Employees, 2002, Velocity Business Publishing

Recruiting Excellence, 2001, Velocity Business Publishing